After gaining a degree in Microbiology at Reading University, Jennifer Meek carried on research at Sussex University and later at Bristol Medical School. She became interested in health and immunity after working in the tropics and subsequently became a qualified nutritionist.

At present she teaches science in a secondary school in Dorset. Her first book *Immune Power* was published by Macdonald Optima in 1990.

SICK EARTH SYNDROME AND HOW TO SURVIVE IT

JENNIFER MEEK

An Optima book

First published in 1992 by
Macdonald Optima, a division of
Macdonald & Co. (Publishers) Ltd
A member of Maxwell Macmillan Publishing Corporation

Macdonald & Co (Publishers) Ltd
165 Great Dover St
London
SE1 4YA

Typeset in Century Schoolbook by
Leaper & Gard Ltd, Bristol, England

Printed and bound in Great Britain by
The Guernsey Press Co Ltd, Guernsey, Channel Islands

DEDICATION

To my two children, Matthew and Jennifer, and the pupils of Ashdown School, where I sometimes teach. May they continue to learn how to appreciate and look after themselves, their families and friends, their community, their environment and their world.

ACKNOWLEDGMENTS

In compiling a non-fiction book the author's job is to gather information from as many reliable sources as possible, to assess this knowledge and to write it up in a form that the readers can understand and will find interesting and useful.

It is impossible to mention everyone's research, but there are a few people whose work or help has been particularly valuable in writing this book: Dr Coleman; Doris Grant; Dr Denis Henshaw, University of Bristol; Glen Linfoot, Head of Science, Ashdown School; Ken Pike; Prof. Rea, Surrey University; Dr C. Smith, Salford University; Dr Neil Ward, Surrey University; Tony Webb and others at the old London Food Commission; Andrew Wille and Clare Wallis, editors, Macdonald. Many thanks.

CONTENTS

Pollution at work and school

Pollution we consume

Conclusion

PREFACE

What does the word 'pollution' mean to you? We all know that we are living in an increasingly polluted world, and that it has become essential to take action to try to reverse this undesirable situation. Pollution, however, does not begin and end with massive global issues that affect each and every one of us, but that we often feel powerless to do anything about; pollution is with us at work, and even our homes cannot be called safe places where we can get away from it all. At work and at home we are bombarded with other people's radio waves and microwaves, as well as other man-made and natural electromagnetic forces. We have to breathe in air pollutants; even the chair we sit on or the bed we sleep in may be a hazard to our health. The foods we eat, the things we drink, the medicines we take, how we move, how we relax, what we think, where and how we live will all determine the quantity and type of pollutants that we contaminate our bodies with.

Technology has zoomed ahead, providing us with new chemicals and machines that we use daily, all having effects on our health and quality of life. We all enjoy many of the comforts of modern living, perhaps so much so that we spend little time thinking about the consequences; but research into the safety and desirability of these new advances is now showing us some of the less desirable side effects. What we need to do is to find that all important balance that will enable us to be healthy in what is at present an unhealthy world; that will enable us to pinpoint the problems that may be affecting us, specifically as individuals, so that we can take steps to rectify or to compensate for them.

This book considers many of the pollution problems that we face in our everyday lives, and offers suggestions on how to deal with them, in the light of current knowledge. Clean-up plans are now, fortunately, being considered throughout the world and are, to some extent, being put into action, although there is no room for complacency. This book also points out what is, perhaps, not so obvious: that we can reduce our own personal pollution and the pollution in our homes and at work, and so reduce our own risk of disease, premature aging and premature death.

We have to start somewhere, and this book shows you where and how. We can all improve our bodies, homes, schools, workplaces, even our world, with a little thought, effort and knowledge, making them safer, healthier and happier places to live in.

POLLUTION IN THE ENVIRONMENT

1
POLLUTION OF MOVEMENT

With our increased technology and division of labour our purity of movement is often destroyed. We have various joints, sets of muscles and organs that were all designed to be used but many of us now follow a sedentary lifestyle, both at work and at home. We go from home to the car; to the office and back in the car; to the television set; and then to bed. This is very restricted movement and not at all what we were intended to do. Paradoxically this sort of existence can make us feel very tired, and even less inclined to exercise.

We need a balance in our movement, as in all other things. People these days can suffer from repetitive strain injury, for example, basically caused by too much use of and pressure on certain muscles – usually the fingers and wrists. Yet the same people often suffer from stiff and degenerating joints, simply because they do not use most of them enough; they are constantly sitting cramped up and inactive, using little apart from their keyboard fingers.

The very mention of exercise often increases the desire to put your feet up and have a cup of tea. We are not aiming at top athlete training or maximum physical capacity. What we want to do is to move easily and without pain for as much of our lives as possible and so be able to enjoy life to the full. This means avoiding pollution of movement, and restoring that purity of movement which we are all capable of achieving.

WHAT CAN WE DO?

General stamina

Firstly we need to consider those vital internal organs such as the heart and lungs. How flexible and capable are they? How well do they cope with doing that little bit extra? We want to be able to run upstairs or after the children without feeling out of breath.

Some form of regular exercise (and by that I mean weekly or preferably daily, not yearly) that increases the heart beat and breathing to a comfortable, but nevertheless, higher level, is required here. Walking briskly for half an hour is fine; if you feel more energetic, cycling, swimming, skipping, jogging, racquet sports or aerobic exercise are also suitable. This form of exercise will not only improve the heart and lungs; it will also improve general stamina, the ability to last out without flagging in normal daily life. It will also improve your feeling of well being by increasing the output of endorphins – the body's natural 'happiness' chemicals.

Breathing

The lungs age quite rapidly compared to other organs, usually through loss of capacity, which is in turn brought about by lack of use. Breathing deeply and properly is vitally important to stop this unnecessary premature degeneration. With loss of lung capacity comes inefficient and insufficient carriage of oxygen to other parts of the body, which in turn can increase the risk of cancer (cancer cells switch to an anaerobic, i.e. without oxygen, form of respiration to obtain their energy). It can also decrease powers of concentration and efficiency, as well as increase feelings of depression.

For those who are less mobile, singing or playing a wind instrument, or even deep and varied breathing can improve this situation.

Aerobic exercise

A sedentary lifestyle, possibly combined with poor

posture, bad work position and tension, increases the necessity for part of the day to be devoted to some form of vigorous exercise. However, while exercise is important, don't overdo it, or you will do more harm than good; remember to build up gradually, not to exercise right on top of a meal and to stop if anything hurts.

It has been suggested that a pulse guide is useful to gauge optimum exercise levels. This involves finding your resting pulse rate (usually by taking your pulse on waking). To this number you add your age, and then subtract the total from 220. You then find 60 per cent and 80 per cent of this figure and add your resting pulse rate to both of these. You now have two figures, a low one and a higher one, between which you should try to keep your pulse rate whilst you are exercising. This is a good guide; it makes sure that you do enough exercise to do some good, but not too much so as to do any harm. As your fitness improves, so your resting pulse rate should go down.

Flexibility

Next we need to feel that we are supple, that we can bend but not break. When we have to sit in a fixed position for long periods of time, muscles can shorten and stiffen, and the flow of lymph around the body slows down. This causes various aches and pains, particularly in the neck – listen to how it creaks when it does circular movements. The lymph cleans up toxins and fights bugs less efficiently, as it needs muscular movement to push it around.

To be flexible we need to keep all of the joints well oiled and mobile. Stretching and bending exercises are necessary to achieve this degree of movement. Massage can also help, especially for those who cannot move easily. Massage, of course, also helps with relaxation and the feelings of well being associated with touch; it is an excellent family activity, which can decrease strain and tension. You can even do it whilst watching the television if you are a TV addict.

Strength and tone

We require strength, not only to lift the children and to pull and push the furniture or the car, but to hold our tummies in, to pump our blood and lymph around, and to look firm and in control of our muscles rather than appearing flabby. It is not necessary to go to regular weight training to achieve strength, although weight-lifting is good for this.

The aim is not to be a champion strong man, but to look firm, to feel fit not weak, to prevent premature muscle degeneration and to have the strength to do all the necessary pulling, pushing and lifting with ease. Sit-ups and press-ups are good for increasing strength, as are cycling and rowing.

Relaxation

On top of all this general all-round movement, we need relaxation, sound sleep and unpolluted dreams.

MOVING NATURALLY

In daily life, try to move naturally more often. Play with the children instead of just organising them; garden more often, or take up some other active hobby. If you don't want a dog, take the children, a friend or even just yourself for a walk. Carry the groceries, unless of course you shop once a week and have an unmanageable amount. Take the stairs rather than the lift or elevator, and perhaps do some of the rougher sawing or other DIY jobs by hand sometimes.

Remember that the way you breathe, the way you sit, stand or lift are vital. Do them the right way and you improve your condition; do them the wrong way and you could end up flat on your back for weeks. Try to find all of your muscles, and use them all sometimes. Many muscles can be exercised whilst we do mundane things; you can relax and contract stomach muscles, repeatedly raise yourself on to tiptoe and lower yourself again, and even contract and relax the female pelvic floor whilst standing washing up or peeling the vegetables.

If you are going to sit and watch TV after a relatively sedentary day, simple stretching and bending exercises can be done in the comfort of your chair. If you really need to sit and relax, however, at least sit properly so that you do not crush your stomach and give yourself indigestion, or cross your legs and impair circulation, or slouch and strain your back.

The way you move throughout your life says a lot about how you are and how you will be in years to come.

2
POLLUTION OF THE MIND

Just as we are what we eat, drink and breathe, so we are what we think. Our minds and personalities are built up out of the thoughts with which they are fed and on which they dwell. It is as easy to pollute the mind as it is to pollute the air, food and water. For example, people who, often without realising it, cultivate unhealthy, negative and distressing thoughts are generally more prone to mental and physical illness than those who dwell on happier, more positive thoughts. Polluted thinking can be just as devastating to the body as environmental pollution. Fortunately, however, we do have some control over what we fill our minds with, and can choose the healthier options.

I shall always remember one English literature project at school, when we studied the works of Edgar Alan Poe, the writer of weird and often frightening short stories and poems with strange meanings, mystical significance and horrific effects. I remember thinking that, great writer though he is proclaimed to be, I was very glad that I didn't have such a vivid and terrible imagination. In order to write you have to think about the story and the feelings expressed within it, and I concluded that I would not have liked to dwell on such awful thoughts for long, even knowing that they were only in the imagination. It was not until later that I learned of Poe's perverse life, his addiction to alcohol, his depression, his dissipated lifestyle, his continual dwelling on premonitions that he would come to a hopeless end, and the fact that he killed himself when he was only 41. Morbid, frightening, distressful, hateful, helpless and unhappy thoughts can be just as toxic as alcohol, cigarettes and drugs when they are taken to excess.

Life has many problems, so it is not always possible to be on top of the world. But it is not so much the problems as our attitudes towards them that determine whether we come through each stress or drown in our sorrows. It is all very well suggesting changing thought patterns to happier thoughts, but quite another thing to do it if you have suffered bereavement or are desperately worried about a job loss, financial problems or ill health. Such suggestions must nevertheless be made, because, unless the thought is actually put into a depressed person's head, they are unlikely to think of it themselves. It often takes a determined effort to try to balance upsetting thoughts with more pleasant ones, and it can be harder than trying to change your diet.

WHAT WE CAN DO

Balance

We need to be able to balance whatever life throws at us with constructive thoughts and actions. Obviously we all have to cope with bereavements, disappointments and pain at various times – events that will make us unhappy. Indeed, it is necessary to feel unhappy when sad things happen; we would be very cold and uncaring individuals if we felt nothing at all. But although we need to feel sad, we should not dwell on these sad feelings all of the time. Life goes on, and a balance can be found.

Choice

Every day we have the choice: we can make the best of that day; we can do only what we have to do; or we can waste the day completely. The choice is always ours.

It is a good idea, every day, to try to do something that you want to do as opposed to that which you have to do; to smile; to be enthusiastic; to think beautiful thoughts for some of the time; even if you are being given a diet of ugly or negative problems. It is vital to believe in yourself, even if you are being put down. Opinion is, after all, only relative. So know and trust your own instincts and abilities and never lose your sense of humour.

YOU ARE WHAT YOU THINK

We know that changes in our thought patterns can bring about physical and emotional changes. With positive thinking we can increase our white blood cell count and improve the immune system and resistance to infection. Depression brings about the reverse. Some women even believe that they are pregnant when they are not, their bodies altering as if they were; of course, they do not give birth with this false pregnancy, but the physical changes are quite real.

Pollution of the mind can thus cause very real physical and emotional problems. So it is that a continual diet of violent videos, for example, or hateful thoughts, are not to be encouraged. Even thinking of nothing very much can alter the personality, making it boring, bored and often lazy. Habitual negative thoughts can bring about addiction and anti-social behaviour. The mind needs exercise; creative daydreaming is not a waste of time, and the more beautiful thoughts that can be taken in, the more pleasure can be brought by recalling these at a later date.

Look for and recognise polluted thoughts, and replace them whenever possible. Make sure that you are in control of your thoughts and your life and that they are not controlling you. At least think about it.

3
POLLUTION OF
THE BODY

How well do you feel?

Do you wake most mornings refreshed and full of enthusiasm for the day ahead? Do you go to work looking good and feeling good, with a smile on your face; or do you drag yourself there, clothes flung on in haste, wearing a harrassed expression and facing the work, the people and the pressures with a certain amount of dread?

Does your body work well and painlessly, or does it creak, groan and hurt when you ask it to do that little bit extra? Do you often feel depressed, lethargic, irritable or tense? Are headaches, backache, PMT, allergies or infections frequent companions? Obviously none of us feels wonderful all of the time, but we should most of the time. Remember, it is the attitude with which we cope with problems that determines whether we make the most out of the problems and pleasures of life or whether life becomes a trial.

Most of us spend hours every day working to earn money. We also spend a considerable amount of time cleaning our homes and possessions. But little thought or time is spent, in comparison, on repairing, cleaning and maintaining our bodies, even though we are stuck with the same model all of our lives − there is no trading-in a body for one that is in better condition!

FOOD

We often eat from habit, when it's time to eat, e.g. during a designated lunch break, or when we have time to grab a snack. On many occasions little thought is given as to whether the food stuffed in is what we need, whether it will do any good except to fill the gap or whether it will do any harm.

Does the food we eat contain all of the nutrients necessary to keep us healthy? Does it contain a whole heap of artificial, or indeed natural, chemicals that are undesirable and likely to put the body's normal biochemistry out of balance? These questions will be addressed later in the food section of the book.

CHEMICALS

Most of us use domestic cleaners and chemicals of various kinds – cosmetics, medicines, DIY and gardening chemicals. These will also be dealt with in their own sections later, but we should always remember that they all have the ability to pollute our bodies if we let them. There is a lot that we can do to avoid contamination, to avoid some chemicals altogether and to use those that are necessary in such a way that exposure is minimal.

Pollution is cumulative; we may not notice the effects whilst we are young, but as we get older and increase our body's burdens, the toxic effects start to show. One of the main secrets of growing old slowly, gracefully and least painfully is to keep out as many pollutants as possible. We can never avoid everything, but the more slowly we build up toxic metals, pesticides or whatever, the longer we can live without being troubled by their accumulation and side effects.

BODY REPAIR AND MAINTENANCE

The cleaner and better maintained we are, both inside and out, the longer we are liable to stay in good condition.

Polluted bodies cloud our outlook on life. They are often not physically sick enough to make us take the week off and say that we are ill, but they may be sick enough to make us feel that we could enjoy life more if we felt better. Mentally and emotionally, we are not necessarily totally blind, but the view is cloudy enough that we cannot see our way through life clearly and so often stumble, get lost or waste time and opportunity.

BEING IN CONTROL

We function best when we feel in control of body and mind and the situations we find ourselves in; when we have confidence in ourselves and our abilities.

It is relatively easy to spot a person who has this control and confidence. They may not have great wealth or position, or whatever you regard as a sign of success. Instead they have more than this: a clear direction in life; a body that is held and moved with pride and ease; a charisma which is not dependent on expensive clothes nor obvious good looks. They smile genuine smiles with their eyes as well as their mouths, and speak and act with confidence. They are in control, even when there are problems.

BODY LAB

The body is a complex living laboratory. It is easily polluted by the air it breathes in, the food and drink it consumes, the chemicals with which it comes into contact, and all forms of radiation. The good news is that we have a built-in repair system, as long as we don't overload it; we can detoxify some pollutants, and avoid others. With a little knowledge and effort we can minimise body pollution and look and feel good for most of the time.

4
POLLUTION OF WATER

Water is essential for many life processes. It is needed to extract water-soluble nutrients from our food and it is used in most of the body's chemistry. All of the water-soluble poisons and wastes that accumulate in the body are excreted in solution, be it as tears, sweat or urine. It is essential to life.

We get a lot of the water we need from the food we eat, but the rest we obtain from what we drink. Water pollution has always been a problem, and water-borne diseases have killed many people in the past. Nowadays, though, we have effective water treatment which kills most of the bacteria responsible for disease; instead we have the problem of chemical pollution.

All of our water is recycled, either by man or naturally in the water cycle; we do not get new, clean water every time it rains. Rainwater has been evaporated from the seas, rivers, lakes and streams; it is, of course, a lot cleaner than water taken directly from a river, but air pollution has made sure that it gets its fair share of dirt.

Water recycled by man often contains a lot of contaminants. It may contain lead, aluminium, mercury, cadmium, glass, plastics, pesticides, fertilisers, detergents, medicines, oil, and a whole host of other chemical compounds, all of which may react together to form an undesirable chemical cocktail. Some areas, where water is obtained from boreholes, have quite clean, relatively uncontaminated water, but others where water comes from surface sources may not be so good, and some is really dreadful and badly contaminated, depending on the type of work in the area.

Water authorities will now give you a general analysis of the water in your area, as a result of which you may be pleasantly surprised or you may decide to use an additional form of water treatment at home.

WATER PURIFICATION AT HOME

Distillation
This will remove almost everything except volatile organic compounds like the chlorine compounds – these evaporate off first and go into the collecting vessel before the water, which joins it later. This type of treatment is very expensive to run, usually unnecessary, and in any case removes the minerals in water, like calcium and magnesium, that are positively beneficial.

Filters
These also do not remove chlorine compounds, nor a lot of the other dissolved chemicals. Fabrics or ceramic filters are really only effective at removing particles and organisms.

Charcoal filters are good for waters that have an unpleasant taste or smell, as they can usually remove these, along with some of the volatile organic compounds, solvents and oils. As with any filter, however, it is important to change the charcoal filter element frequently, as it is difficult to tell when the filter is no longer effective (they clog up easily, especially in hard water areas where there is a lot of calcium and magnesium in the water). Filters can also be good breeding grounds for bacteria if they are not kept clean and so can provide their own health risk if not looked after properly.

Boiling
Boiling for 10 minutes or so will kill most bugs and also reduce, but not totally eliminate, volatile organic compounds.

Reverse osmosis

Reverse osmosis is an effective way of removing solvents, pesticides, chlorine, volatile organics and minerals from otherwise clean water. A membrane of nylon, acetate or cellulose is used, but as it is very fine, it clogs up very quickly if the water contains solid material.

Water softeners

Water softeners should not be used for drinking water as salt (sodium chloride) is used in these and obviously dissolves in the water. It is not good to take in too much sodium, and so it is better to leave a tap untreated for drinking and cooking water, even if a softener is used to protect your water heater and washing machine.

Other important points

- It is always a good idea to run your tap for a few minutes first thing in the morning, if making tea or coffee. Water standing in the pipes overnight is much more likely to have taken up contaminants, especially if your pipes are lead or copper and the water is soft.
- Do not drink water from the hot water tap as it will have been stored in the hot water tank and may well contain quite high levels of copper or aluminium, in particular.
- Do not use aluminium or copper saucepans for cooking acidic foods, as these elements easily dissolve into the water. Glass or stainless steel pans are much less likely to cause contamination.
- If you know that your water is high in an undesirable element like fluoride, aluminium, lead, cadmium, etc., try to avoid other additional sources of these.
- If you are using a water filter, remember to change it frequently.
- If you are using bottled water, remember that, once opened, it can become contaminated quite quickly. Don't keep it for ages.

Water is our most essential nutrient; we need unpolluted water.

5
LAND
POLLUTION

It has been said that man is the only suicidal animal. He is the only animal to make such a concerted effort to poison the air he breathes, the food he eats, the water he drinks and the land he needs to live on.

The earth has been around for about 5 billion years. Man is a relative newcomer, but he has certainly made his mark. Just like vandals scrawling graffiti over public places, he has scrawled all over the land. His demolition of forests has not only wounded the land but has also had far-reaching effects on air quality. He has carelessly scarred the landscape with mines in order to obtain the oil, coal and minerals that he desires. He had poured poisons over the land under the covering umbrella of improving agriculture. Unbalanced but cheap fertilisers encourage the growth of nutrient-deficient crops, and pesticides kill anything that might try to share the harvest. Probably worst of all is the disposal of waste – on the land, under the land, in the seas and waters, and in the air.

At present, some land is so toxic that it cannot be built on, or even played near because of the fumes it gives off and the dangers of contamination. Some land is not fit to grow crops on or to graze animals on because nearby industrial waste would poison these living things.

We as individuals have little power over these major activities, but we can, collectively, work towards a local, national and even worldwide clean-up. Most of us do not want to live in a slum; this world can be a beautiful place, and we should all try to look after it and keep it that way.

WHAT WE CAN DO

- Support moves to encourage industry, agriculture, etc., to clean up their waste before they dump it.
- If you use them at all, use household and garden chemicals with care, and only when necessary. Remember that anything that is designed to kill living things, be it '99 per cent of household germs' or the tiny blackfly, is intended to destroy life and is therefore bound to have some effect on you too.
- Use environmentally friendly products in preference to those that do damage.
- Think about your rubbish. For example don't put old medicines down the loo, as the water is recycled. Don't thrown rubbish away as litter, wherever you are; old bottles and cans can be dangerous to many living things, as well as looking unsightly.
- Recycle things like aluminium cans, bottles, vegetable waste, paper, etc.

RECYCLING

It has been estimated that every 2½ tons of rubbish could produce as much energy as 1 ton of coal. However, less than 10 per cent of our rubbish is used to produce energy.

Glass

We use more than 6 billion jars and bottles every year in Britain; it is one of the safest forms of packaging. The glass from these discarded bottles can be crushed, melted and used again. Every ton of broken glass could save 150 litres of oil, as well as replace raw materials.

Metals

Cans and other scrap metal like aluminium, copper, gold, iron, lead, silver and tin could all be melted down and reused, so saving some of that mining. Again, it takes a lot of oil to make things like aluminium cans, but it takes much less if the metal is reused.

Car tyres and engine oil

Tyres can be recycled and used as fillers or in paints. Old car oil, too, should be taken to a garage when you have finished with it; it can be recycled, which is far better than putting it down the drain, where it can cause a lot of pollution problems.

Organic waste

Vegetable food waste can be used as compost if you have a garden.

Animal manure is still very abundant but considered less desirable than cheap and clean artificial fertilisers. It would be better used as a fertiliser rather than dumped in concentrated quantities in rivers, where it pollutes our water.

Plastics

Plastics are best kept separate from everything else; once mixed with other waste they cannot easily be separated. They are often not biodegradable, and so make a mess for a long time.

Wood and its products

Paper, wood and cardboard can all be sorted, shredded and reused in some form or another. Recycled paper usually has to be mixed with some new paper to make it acceptable in quality, but this is all right as trees are planted specifically for paper-making; they are quick growing, and constantly replanted to keep up the supply. The young trees on these plantations are also good for the air, as a young tree takes up around three times as much carbon oxides as older trees and produces oxygen.

The costs of recycling

Unfortunately it is often more expensive, and definitely more time consuming, to recycle than it is to use new raw materials. We therefore need to become more efficient at recycling. It is also much more expensive to render toxic waste harmless than it is to dump it somewhere out of the way; nevertheless we must try, we must start somewhere.

The land grows our food. We cannot afford to poison it.

6
POLLUTION OF OUR ATMOSPHERE

The atmosphere is more than just a mixture of gases, water vapour, dust and dirt; it is the shield that protects our earth from things in space, like meteorites, which might crash into it; the shield that protects us from the sun's harmful radiation; the provider of our weather. It supports all life on earth.

The air that we breathe is that part of our atmosphere which immediately surrounds us, that is closest to the earth's surface. Above it comes the troposphere, then the stratosphere, the ionosphere and the exosphere. All exist in a balance, but that balance is now being destroyed by human activity and its consequent pollution.

CLIMATE

Our earth is getting too warm, and this is upsetting our climatic conditions. The mean temperature of the earth today is the highest ever recorded, and a further rise is inevitable in the future. It is possible that this may cause a rise in the sea level as glaciers and ice sheets melt, which could in turn wipe out some low-lying areas and islands. It will certainly increase the occurrence of hurricanes and other extreme weather conditions, and will alter our climatic zones.

Greenhouse effect
Greenhouse gases are those gases in the atmosphere that allow the sun's heat to reach the earth's surface, but which

also slow down its subsequent escape. These gases, in the correct amounts, are essential to life on earth as we know it. Without the greenhouse gases the earth would be too cold – too much of the sun's heat would escape. But with too high a concentration of the greenhouse gases the earth would get too hot – not enough of the sun's heat would be able to escape. We therefore need to keep the balance right.

At present we are producing too many greenhouse gases. There are about 30 in all, but the main ones are the carbon oxides, produced during the combustion of fossil fuels; and methane, produced by rotting vegetation, as a byproduct of mining, and as flatulence from ruminating cattle.

To reduce the production of greenhouse gases, therefore, we have to decrease the pollution caused by the burning of fossil fuels, although this will be expensive. We can change to less polluting fuels and energy sources like wind, wave and solar power which are viable less-polluting alternatives in some situations. We can use less fuel by using it more efficiently, e.g. make more use of public transport. We can prevent the greenhouse gases from entering the atmosphere by planting more trees and restricting the destruction of forests such as the tropical rainforests.

THE OZONE LAYER

The protective ozone layer in the stratosphere is being destroyed, so threatening our health and indeed our survival.

A molecule of oxygen, O_2, consists of two oxygen atoms. In the stratosphere oxygen is exposed to the sun's ultraviolet radiation, which splits the oxygen molecules into their constituent atoms. These atoms, with a catalyst, can combine to form ozone, O_3, the ozone is then split by the ultraviolet radiation, and so the process continues. The important feature of the chain reaction is that it absorbs ultraviolet radiation. It is this same chain reaction that gases such as CFCs (chloroflourocarbons) interrupt, causing the thinning of, and holes, in the ozone layer.

Ultraviolet radiation in large doses is a sterilising agent, while in lower doses it can increase the risk of harmful genetic changes in all living things – an increase in skin cancers is the best-publicised risk to humans. So if too much ultraviolet were to reach the earth's surface it would increase the risk of damage to all forms of life and could even destroy life altogether. Even with a thinner ozone layer, some plants and animals would have problems; we already have evidence of the ozone hole causing an increase in the incidence of cataracts and skin cancer in humans, as well as causing damage in plankton and other marine life.

Ozone at ground level
We also need to prevent the build up of ozone down here in the air we breathe. Ozone is very toxic when breathed in – not surprising when you realise it is used commercially as a bleaching agent and germicide. It is ironic that something that is so toxic to us directly, provides us with the protection we need from the ultraviolet radiation that could destroy all living things.

Ozone is produced by electrical discharges; these occur naturally (lightning) and artificially (high-voltage electrical equipment). It is also produced by the action of sunlight on pollutants such as the exhaust fumes of cars.

ACID RAIN

All rain is slightly acid; for example it contains small amounts of carbon dioxide, present as carbonic acid. But acid rain is rain in which the acidity is considerably higher than usual – in some cases as much as 1,000 times more acid than it would normally be. It appears to be caused by dissolved sulphur compounds produced by industrial pollution, particularly from power stations.

Acid rain is damaging the earth's waters and forests. It is also releasing other pollutants, like free aluminium, into our waters, compounding its toxic effect. Fish may then contain far higher levels of contaminating metals than they would if living in less acidic waters. Animals, too, including humans, tend to concentrate this extra metallic burden which they have picked up from the food they eat, whether it be plant or animal. They then need far higher concentrations of the nutritional minerals to balance and compensate for this.

OTHER ATMOSPHERIC POLLUTANTS

Other dangerous chemicals in the air – chemicals such as dioxins, lead from petrol, and by-products of disposing of or burning toxic and chemical waste – are poisoning plant and animal life.

PCBs (polychlorinated bi-phenyls) have been found to be so dangerous that it is now illegal to find new uses for them in Europe. However there are still some 200,000 tonnes in existence, all of which will need to be disposed of somehow. Quite often such waste is burned at sea, on board special waste-disposal ships, but although this is less irritating than burning it on land, it doesn't help the atmosphere at all.

We must look after all of our atmosphere, not only the part we breathe.

7
POLLUTION OF THE AIR

Breathing is essential to human life. We take about 14 to 18 breaths every minute whilst sitting still. However, even in a relatively clean place, we can take in around 40,000 specks of dust every time we breathe, and in a dirty atmosphere we can take in many thousands more, sometimes with disastrous consequences. For example, just prior to the passing of the UK's Clean Air Act in December 1956, 1,000 people died in a smog incident; four years previously the death toll had been 4,000.

We do have defence mechanisms which prevent some of this dirt from entering the lungs, but these are just not sufficient to cope with the size and nature of today's pollution. As individuals we cannot clean up the air, but we can lend our voice and support to those who are trying to do this. We can also contribute in some ways to the major clean-up by improving our own mini-atmospheres and environments.

WHAT WE CAN DO

- Plants are the best air improvers. We can plant trees to help the environment, especially if we live on a busy street. We can also have plants in our homes and workplaces; these help to reduce internal air pollution.
- We can try not to use cars unnecessarily, and not to leave the engine running when we don't need it. Schools are some of the worst areas for this; parents come to pick up their children and don't switch off the engine

whilst they are waiting. When the children do come out, they plough through a sea of exhaust fumes and take in a hefty lead and benzopyrene supplement before they get their lift home. Running the engine in an integral garage, even with the door open, can pollute the air space in the rooms above.

- Use lead-free petrol if possible and watch out for the new catalytic converters that remove some of the other pollutants as well.
- Make sure cookers, boilers, etc., are clean and well ventilated so that fewer fumes are created and breathed in.
- Be aware of household and DIY materials; keep lids on whenever possible; use brushes or roll-ons rather than aerosols.
- Don't smoke, or, if you really cannot give it up, at least respect other people's right to have smoke-free air, and don't smoke in a non-smoker's house or place of work.
- Do not irresponsibly throw out old fire extinguishers, fridges or anything which contains refrigerant gases, solvents or other toxic chemicals.

We all have to share the air. We often take it for granted because we cannot see it, but we cannot live without it and the cleaner it is the better.

8
NOISE POLLUTION

We become so accustomed to some noises that we only notice them when they stop but other noises are essential because we use them for communication. We have adapted to tolerate noise levels involved in normal speech, but it can be very damaging to shout in someone's ear.

Noise is thus any sort of sound, although we usually use the word to describe a sound that we find disturbing, unpleasant or just plain too loud. Although one person's noise may be another's music, there is no doubt that sounds which are too loud, even if they are music, are damaging.

A loud bang can damage many of the hair cells that detect sound in our cochlea (inner ear), and, once damaged, these will not be replaced. Loud noises can also cause constriction of tiny blood vessels throughout the whole body. Specifically, if the inner ear is deprived of blood, there may be further destruction of the cells responsible for hearing.

Noise damage is cumulative. We may not notice any obvious damage after going to a very loud concert, but if we are continually in this environment, hearing damage may result. Several members of famous rock bands have suffered from this problem later in life.

Some animals hear sounds above those that we hear. In contrast, some sounds are so low we do not really hear them at all, but feel them in the stomach and chest; this type of sound has even been used as a form of riot control.

Noise is potentially damaging to all things, it can even shatter glass. Yet today's society creates more and more noise – cars and planes, boats and trains, mowers and vacuum cleaners, washing machines and freezers, saws and drills, televisions and radios, record players, cassettes, walkmans, discos and bands. Entertainment, industry, transport and recreation all seem to need noise.

Noise can also cause ill health by disturbing sleep. A fridge or central heating coming on and going off at various times during the night may take more of a toll on our beauty sleep than we realise. It can also over-stimulate us whilst we are awake, draining us of mental and physical energy throughout the day. It is thought that noisy classrooms can provoke learning disorders as well as behavioural problems. Excessive noise can lead to aggression, anger and even fear; it can make us tired, tense and irritable.

WHAT CAN WE DO ABOUT IT?

- Always use ear protectors when they are deemed necessary for your job. You can probably tolerate the noise and feel that you can do without them as noise does not always hurt. However, noise damage is cumulative; it is better to protect your hearing now and prevent hearing loss later in life.
- Turn personal equipment, stereos, walkmans, TVs and the like down to a sensible volume, instead of seeing just how loud you can stand it.
- Close doors at night and arrange furniture, etc., so that fridges, freezers, boilers and other equipment that make noises do not interfere with your sleep.
- Noise can make you very tired, so make sure that you have some periods of silence throughout the day.
- If you live on a busy street or near an airport, install double-glazing to cut down the noise.
- If you live in a terraced or a semi-detached house, and your neighbours are noisy, place bookcases or similar pieces of furniture against your shared walls, as these absorb sounds.

9
LIGHT
POLLUTION

Man would normally live and work in natural light, with periods of light and darkness. Nowadays, however, especially in winter, we may live in artificial light most of the time, and extend our periods of light for as long as we want. Schools and workplaces often have row upon row of fluorescent striplights.

Unfortunately this harsh continual light has been shown to be very stressful. Furthermore, living in a natural light deficiency can cause bone and muscle weakness, a less effective immune system and a reduction in the body's ability to heal. This is because ordinary lightbulbs are deficient in the blue end of the light spectrum, and light in this region is known to promote healing, and possibly reduce blood pressure.

Artificial lighting is also thought to contribute towards the onset of hyperactivity and other behavioural and learning problems in children. School studies show that children work better in natural light, but natural light is very important for children in other ways. It is needed, in particular, to stimulate the production of growth hormones and to stimulate the immune system, so lessening childhood ailments. Artificial light, in contrast, is known to increase feelings of tiredness as well as depression.

Daylight, as opposed to direct sunlight and artificial light, is thus very beneficial to health. Direct sunlight, however, can be a problem if you get too much of it. It can cause sunburn, and the more often you burn, the more likely you are to develop skin cancer later in life. Sunlight around midday is more harmful than sunlight early and late in the day as it contains more of the harmful ultra-violet B.

SAD

Seasonal affective disorder, or SAD as it is called, is thought to affect half a million people in Britain. SAD people become very tired and depressed in winter, because their bodies are sensitive to natural light deficiency. They eat more and sleep more and do not improve with fluorescent striplighting – they need daylight.

WHAT WE CAN DO

- Make sure that you get some natural daylight every day, especially on the eyes. This is particularly important for people who usually wear glasses or contact lenses, and those suffering from arthritis.
- Be careful with exposure to direct sunlight during the period around midday. Do not allow yourself to burn.
- Work in natural light wherever possible.
- Do not use fluorescent striplighting.
- When choosing or altering a home, make sure that it is light and bright. A light, bright home is more conducive to feeling well: it improves efficiency and personal energy.
- When decorating your home, use stimulating colours like reds and oranges where you expect to do the most work or activity. Use the more peaceful greens and healing blues where you expect to be able to rest.
- Natural light is free, good for your health and doesn't cause pollution.

10
RADON
AS A
POLLUTANT

We are all exposed to natural radiation; we get it from the cosmic rays which reach earth, and from the earth itself, which gives off gamma and alpha radiation. Alpha radiation from the ground is due to the radioactive decay of uranium and thorium, both of which occur naturally in the soil and rocks, and which decay to give a number of other elements including radioactive radon. Some rocks contain more thorium and uranium than others, which accounts for the nationwide variations in radon levels.

RADON GAS

Radon gas is probably our biggest single source of exposure to natural radiation. Radon has a halflife of 3.8 days, i.e. its radioactivity falls to half its original value in 3.8 days. As a gas it is able to move freely out of the soil and into the air, where it tends to accumulate in ground-floor rooms and, in particular, in basements of buildings. People living in high rise flats are less exposed.

The radon gas itself is chemically inert, but it is radio active. The average level of radioactivity in any home is about 20 $Bq.m^{-3}$; this is considered to be a safe background level of radioactivity. It is thought by the experts that if radon gas gives a house a radioactivity reading above 200 $Bq.m^{-3}$ further tests should be carried out, and remedial action taken if then thought to be required.

You are more likely to have high radon levels in the home if:

- You live in one of the high-risk areas where rocks are known to give off a lot of this gas. The granite in the Devon and Cornwall areas produces higher radon concentrations than Scottish granite.
- If you live or work in a basement.
- If you live on the ground floor and the floors are not suspended and are cracked.
- If your house has stone – particularly granite – walls.
- If your house is well-insulated and double-glazed, because this holds the radon in, as well as the heat.
- If your central heating draws more radon up from the ground and into your house.
- If your house is built on very dry land, as radon concentrations can be as much as five times higher from dry soil than from wet soil.

Paradoxically, radon levels are often lower in houses during the summer than they are during the winter. This is probably due to the increased heating and decreased ventilation (closed doors and windows) that we favour during the winter months. Radon levels are usually higher at night for the same reason, i.e. we close our doors and windows for security, especially if living in a bungalow.

The risks from radon gas

Excessive radon exposure has been linked to cancer, in particular to cancer of the lung, kidney, prostate and skin, as well as to leukaemia and childhood cancers.

Back in the 16th century a scientific paper linked lung cancer in mine workers with a gas found in the mines. It was not until the early 1900s that radon gas was identified, but it is now definitely considered to be responsible for cases of lung disease in underground workers who have to breathe in this gas. Radon has not been definitely linked with lung cancer when exposed in the home, however, except where the sufferer was also a smoker, and in such cases it is difficult to tell whether it was the gas or the cigarettes that caused the problem.

Cancer of the prostate is strongly linked with radon, as this gland seems to accumulate radon over a period of time, the slow but continual exposure appearing to do the damage. Repeated exposure to high background levels of radiation carries a far higher risk than one exposure to a massive dose of radiation; for example, the atomic bombs dropped on Japanese cities did not seem to cause an increase in the incidence of this type of cancer.

The kidneys are the organs that filter the radon out of the body, and so they are prone to damage and to cancer over long periods of exposure.

Red bone marrow contains fat cells, which are able to dissolve much more radon than the surrounding marrow. Radon emits polonium, another radioactive element, as it decays, and this polonium can enter the blood and lungs and contribute to cancer of both.

Because radon and polonium can accumulate on the skin and so irradiate skin cells (the melanocytes or pigment producers, in particular), it is possible they they could contribute towards cancer of the skin. However it is very difficult to say exactly how great this risk is as it is almost impossible to remove the interaction with exposure to the sun.

What can we do?

The first obvious thing to do is to have your house tested to see if you are exposed to high radon levels or not. This can be done relatively cheaply and easily, using a special type of plastic, a polymer derived from allyl diglycol, which is not sensitive to gamma rays, X-rays, beta particles or visible light, but is sensitive to alpha particles – the radioactivity produced by radon. Many schoolchildren, as part of their study, are now testing for radon using this method. Subsequent analysis of the plastic after it has been in the house for a few months is carried out by a group at Bristol University. The National Radiological Protection Board also carry out tests. If readings are high on preliminary tests, further tests may be required.

If it is then necessary to take remedial steps, the following may be suggested.

- Increased ventilation. This is always a good interim measure, as radon disperses easily and will go out of open windows and doors.
- If it is the middle of winter and you do not want to open all of the windows and doors, fans can be used to exchange air. However such fans should be fitted by someone who is aware of the problem, or you may spend a lot of money having fans fitted which bring radon into the house, rather than removing it; simple extractor fans tend to have this effect.
- It is always better to prevent radon from entering the house rather than trying to get it out again, if at all possible. Cracks and openings to the earth beneath can be sealed. There is now a plastic material available which will do the job, if it is laid properly.
- Air can be pumped out from beneath the house, so that the radon is dispersed.

ELECTROMAGNETIC POLLUTION

11
WHAT IS ELECTRO-MAGNETISM?

Electromagnetic radiation consists of waves of energy, combining electric and magnetic fields. There is an enormous range, or spectrum, of electromagnetic radiation, from very long radio waves at one end to X-rays and gamma rays at the other, with visible light falling in a very narrow waveband somewhere in the middle.

Man has always had a natural background exposure to electromagnetic radiation. All forms of radiation bombard the earth's atmosphere from space; some of this is absorbed by the atmosphere, but the rest reaches the earth's surface. Furthermore, there are natural sources of such radiation here on earth – for example the radioactive elements in the earth's crust produce electromagnetic radiation. And just as nature has made use of the many different atoms and molecules in the construction of living systems, so she has also used combinations of electromagnetic frequencies.

Electromagnetism is thus essential to all living things, to life as we know it. Animals and plants use electromagnetism for communication, regulation and control. Even the earth's electromagnetic field has effects on our physiology and pyschology, as we shall see later.

Man has therefore evolved alongside these naturally occurring electromagnetic frequencies. However, over the last 100 years or so, we have added to this electromagnetic burden, first by the generation of electricity, then with radio transmission, radar, TV, telecommunications, microwave ovens, sunbeds – the list goes on and on. This added burden has to have some effect on our health.

FREQUENCIES

The list below is a very simplified guide to the frequencies that we are exposed to, starting with the very low frequencies and progressing to the high frequencies. It is especially interesting to note that electricity power-lines use frequencies very close to the frequencies of the brain, muscles and nerves. Communications, radio, TV and radar use frequencies between those generated by thunderstorms and infrared radiation. Relative positions in this list give an indication of likely effects on or interference with man's biological systems.

- Solar frequencies.
- Lunar frequencies.
- Earth's rotation; our sleep cycles.
- Normal functions of living things.
- Human heart beat.
- Brainwaves.
- Power supply systems.
- Muscle and nerve potentials.
- Thunderstorms.
- Radio waves, TV, broadcasting and radar.
- Infrared radiation.
- Visible light.
- Ultraviolet radiation.
- Ionising radiation – X-rays, gamma rays.

We are all adapted to solar, lunar and geophysical forces; their effects are imperceptible and considered normal, which, indeed they are. However, we must not lose sight of the fact that they do affect living things. Behaviour may well be altered slightly depending on these forces. For example, schizophrenic and mannic depressive patients show seasonal fluctuations in mood and there is growing concern about the number of people suffering from SAD (seasonal affective disorder), which causes seasonal depression. In March the earth's alignment towards the galactic centre causes stimulation of all living things.

The moon alters the Earth's geomagnetic field during its $29\frac{1}{2}$-day cycle, so that it is greater the nearer one is to the full moon. Weather is supposed to be better around the full moon – some people will only take their holidays then. Bean seeds take up more water just before the full moon, and oysters, kept in the dark, open and close their valves in time with the lunar rhythm. But to complicate matters, the moon also has a $27\frac{1}{2}$-day cycle, and the greatest change in biological systems occurs when these two coincide.

The polarity of the earth's geomagnetic force reverses every 10,000 to 100,000 years, and there are smaller variations in between. What effect this has on living creatures we don't know, but we do know that geomagnetic changes on the earth's surface at dawn triggers activity in plants as they prepare for photosynthesis, and there are physiological changes in men who work on submarines and so are shielded from normal geomagnetic forces for some of the time. Astronauts, too, show changes due to exposure to altered geomagnetic fields. It used to be thought that light was responsible for our circadian rhythms, but research has now shown that they are brought about by weak extremely low-frequency fields.

Natural electromagnetic radiation and naturally occurring cycles thus have very subtle effects on all living things. It is therefore unreasonable to suppose that other electromagnetic fields will have no effect on us at all.

POSITIVE AND NEGATIVE IONS

Electromagnetic radiation can be ionising or non-ionising. Non-ionising does not mean that it doesn't have any effect on living things, or even that it isn't injurious; it just means that it doesn't have enough energy to alter the electric charge of a material.

Frequencies of non-ionising electromagnetic radiation are from the visible light waveband down through infrared, microwave, radar, TV and radio waves, body waves (i.e. electrical signals in the brain, muscles, nerves, etc.), power supply and geophysical oscillations. Ionising radiation is very high frequency – gamma waves and X-rays – and has enough energy to knock electrons out of place on atoms and molecules. This obviously alters the electric charge, and creates a positive ion. If the displaced electrons are picked up by other atoms and molecules, they will produce negative ions.

It is cosmic radiation that breaks up water molecules in this way and gives the air its electric charge; the air we breathe thus contains these charged particles or ions. Country air, sea air, and air near falling water, mountains and plants all have a lot of negative ions, which give us a sense of well being. It is now possible to buy ionisers that increase the negative ions in our homes; early ionisers, however, generated a lot of ozone as well as negative ions, so were not really to be recommended. A fountain or vegetation are probably the best sources of negative ions in built-up areas.

In contrast, positive ion excess is known to contribute towards anxiety, depression and irritability. Air-conditioned buildings may have more positive ions than negative ones, as will the air before a thunderstorm; hence the headaches, etc., experienced by sensitive people before electrical storms and in air-conditioned buildings. Furthermore, it has been reported that underneath power-lines there are excessive positive ions, and that laboratory animals have died after constant exposure, for three months, to these unusual conditions.

12
ELECTRO-MAGNETISM AND MEDICINE

Man has made considerable use of electromagnetic waves. They provide us with music and information via radio and television; we are increasingly dependent on our electrical luxuries and necessities; they can be used in medicine and also, unfortunately, as weapons of war. Man uses transmitters to emit radio waves and aerials to detect them; lights to emit visible light, and cameras to detect them (our own eyes are also detectors of visible light, of course); X-ray tubes to emit X-rays and a photographic plate to detect them; cobalt 60 to emit gamma rays and a Geiger–Müller tube to detect their presence.

There are many useful applications in medicine. X-rays were discovered in 1895 and are now used extensively for diagnostic purposes. Radioactive labelling has become a very important investigative technique, both in the body and the laboratory; as we saw with radon gas, radioactive materials decay into more stable forms, and as they change their chemical structure they emit electrically charged particles and electromagnetic radiation. If harmless radioactive molecules are attached to biochemically active substances, they can then be tracked around the body.

Nuclear magnetic resonance imaging machines are used to sense the electromagnetic oscillations in the atoms and molecules of the body. Abnormalities in these oscillations can then be detected, revealing, among other problems, brain damage (including plaques caused by Alzheimer's disease), tumours and nerve or muscle disease (including multiple sclerosis).

Heat treatment of muscles and joints is possible, using short-wave diathermy. This uses microwaves, but it should be stressed that only certain frequencies must be used and definitely under medical supervision. The thermal effects of such non-ionising radiation can cause severe burning, particularly of tissue that has no pain-sensitive nerve endings and so can't warn you that any burning is occurring. (On no account should anyone experiment with heat treatment using microwave ovens.) Small blood vessels may also be sealed off during surgery, using electrocautery, and tissue can be cut through using electrosurgery.

Man himself emits electrical signals, the strongest ones from muscles and nerves; he has made equipment that will detect and measure some of this electrical activity. An electrocardiogram (ECG) will measure the heart's electrical signals, and an electroencephalogram (EEG) the brain's signals. Electromyography is the study of electrical signals which come from contracting muscles attached to the skeleton although most of the smaller muscles have electrical activity which is very small and not easily measured. An electrogastrogram measures electrical signals coming from the muscles surrounding our internal organs; and electronystagmography detects the electrical movements of the eye muscles when stimulated by light. The electrical activity of the inner ear can also be measured when stimulated by sound.

Electro therapy may be used to induce sleep, and it may also be used to relieve pain or to act as an anaesthetic. Furthermore, electrotherapy can be employed to help those with mental and depressive illnesses, the frequencies of 27.5 Hz, 55 Hz, 110 Hz, 220 Hz, 440 Hz and 880 Hz being the most effective. Our power-supply frequencies are usually 50 Hz or 60 Hz; it would be interesting to know if we would all feel in better spirits if the beneficial 55 Hz was used instead.

13
ELECTRO-MAGNETISM AND MAN

The detection of an electric potential, i.e. a voltage difference, across a cell membrane is a good indication that the cell is alive. Live biological membranes can have quite high voltage differences across them, and this electrical potential organises all the molecules inside the cell, enabling the body to work.

DISEASE

It is possible that disease could be induced by electromagnetic imbalances, just as it can be caused by viruses, bacteria, poisons, etc. It is also known that excessive exposure to electromagnetic radiation is cumulative in effect, and that it can take several years before symptoms are felt.

Cancer cells have a different capacity for detecting and receiving electrical signals than do healthy tissue, and some research is being carried out to see if electrical stimulation can be used to normalise inoperable tumours.

THE HEAD

The head is that part of us that appears to be the main detector of electromagnetic fields, and the pineal gland in the centre of the brain is probably the most sensitive region within the head. The pineal is also the gland that regulates body functions, depending not only on the light/ dark cycle, but also on the strength of and changes in the earth's geomagnetic fields and on manmade electrical and magnetic fields.

Any disruption in the body's circadian rhythms – the processes affected by the 24-hour day–night cycle – will affect the concentrations of two important brain chemicals, serotonin and melatonin. These changes, in turn, will alter mood, and have been linked to depressive illness. Jet lag may also be attributed to changes in extremely low-frequency fields, and research suggests that taking a supplement of melatonin before the homeward journey may overcome this problem.

OTHER TISSUES

All of our tissues are electrolytic conductors of electricity, i.e. electrical impulses are transmitted and conducted in the fluids within and around the cells of our body. Indeed, it is by this means that many of our biochemicals are transported around the body. In cases where an individual has a fault in this conduction system, it is usually impossible to rectify the problem. However, there are exceptions; for example if there is a problem with the electrical triggering of the heart, an electronic pacemaker can be implanted, usually with a two-year battery, to trigger the pumping action. With this simple electrical fault artificially corrected, the individual can lead a normal life.

Bones

Bone appears to respond to electrical stimulation. It was first observed that salamanders could regenerate a lost limb if an electric current was applied to the area; research has shown that the current flow in the skin altered when there was an injury, and it was deduced that this was part of the healing process. Although, when experiments were carried out on frogs, these animals did not regenerate their limbs, it was found that implanting small electrical batteries in their bodies did increase their ability both to make and to repair bone, cartilage and muscle.

Studies were taken further, applying electrical currents to human bone fractures. It is now possible to help heal some difficult bone fractures by electrical stimulation, but this technique must be used properly – it will certainly not benefit healthy tissue. In fact, if a beneficial current is reversed for any reason, it can cause tissue degeneration.

It is also possible that rubbing an injury, as we instinctively tend to do, may increase the electrical stimulation in the area, so aiding healing.

Blood cells
White blood cells, and in particular the lymphocytes, the cells involved in immune protection, are very sensitive to electromagnetic radiation. This is one of the reasons why there is so much concern over exposure to man-made sources of electromagnetic radiation, and may explain the possible increased risk of leukaemia in those areas where such exposure is high, e.g. around power lines.

Blood lipids
It has been found that over-exposure to alternating magnetic fields, as found around power lines and electrical equipment, causes a build-up of serum triglycerides – one of the fats found in the bloodstream that has been implicated in heart disease. Constant or frequent exposure to such electromagnetic fields could therefore be a contributary factor in the onset of heart disease.

Skin
Skin, like all the body tissues, has an electrical resistance. When it is really dry it has a high resistance; you will feel a considerable shock from the 240-volt (U.K.) domestic supply should you have an accident with it, but it probably wouldn't kill you. However, the same voltage could kill you if the skin was very wet, as water decreases its resistance. Even sweat will decrease the skin's resistance to varying degrees.

Nerves

Nerve impulses travel along a nerve fibre by an electro-chemical process. Although the nervous system is basically electrical in action, a nerve isn't quite like a wire in an electrical circuit; there are many breaks along the length of a nerve; what travels through nerves is therefore not like ordinary electricity that you get in the mains. It is more like a series of tiny electrical leaks passing along the fibres, in a chain reaction. Nerve gases have a paralysing effect because they block the passage of a nerve trans-mitter (acetylcholine) and so prevent transmission of messages.

The brain consists of an enormous network of nerve cells linked together, giving almost limitless potential permutations and combinations. Within the brain, our short-term memory is probably due to an electrochemical process, whereas long-term memory is made possible through chemical change.

BEHAVIOUR

It is known that exposure to strong magnetic and electro-magnetic fields alters mood (causing depression), concentration and behaviour; and it is being researched as a tool for crowd control. It is also thought to increase one's risk of getting cancer, as we have seen.

ALLERGIES

Exposure to excessive electromagnetic fields is believed to sensitise some people so that they become allergic to various things. But sometimes it is the other way around, and people with existing allergies become electromagnetic-ally hypersensitive.

OUR POWER SUPPLY

As should be apparent by now, many of our control functions are automatic by nature – the beating of our heart, our blood pressure, our digestion, from gut movements to control of blood sugar, and other muscular movements – and are all dependent on a sort of electrical supply, a power supply within the body. If something goes wrong with this power supply – perhaps a disruption or interference – problems are going to occur that will be difficult to rectify.

14
POWER SUPPLY

It should be obvious by now that our bodies – indeed those of all living things – utilise electromagnetic forces in order to function and exist. However, just as most of us have the problem of eating too much food (although insufficient essential nutrients), so we are also possibly facing the problem of too much exposure to electromagnetic radiation.

ELECTRICITY

We need electricity; electricity has become such an integral part of 20th-century life that it is difficult to imagine living without it. We therefore have to have either overhead or underground cables in order to supply this electricity. There are, however, problems with such cables which should be considered, both by the authorities when installing them and by the individual when buying property, or considering work, near them.

Health effects
It is now known that health effects due to extremely low-frequency electromagmetic radiation are both time related and cumulative. For example, it may take around six years for people to present with symptoms as a result of exposure to such electromagnetic radiation; but there may be a few who are already stressed to the point of overload, who will present with symptoms almost immediately. Usual symptoms are any combination of:
- Headaches.
- Lack of energy.
- Mental blocks and poor concentration.
- Insomnia, yet falling asleep at other inappropriate times.

- Palpitations.
- Dizziness.
- Trembling.
- Loss of appetite or rashes.
  Later, after longer exposure, symptoms may progress to:
- Blackouts.
- Nervous disorders like depression; feelings of being trapped; anxiety attacks, or suicides.
- Epilepsies.
- Lowered fertility.
- Symptoms of diseases like cancer and arthritis.

These symptoms occur with many illnesses, so it will always be difficult to state categorically that they are caused by electromagnetic overload, e.g. from power lines. As there does appear to be a definite increase in the incidence of these symptoms in the vicinity of power lines, it would seem prudent to keep people out of their direct range in any future planning.

Electromagnetic radiation, comparable to that generated by powerlines, is also known to increase the activity of an enzyme, ornithine decarboxylase, which speeds up the growth of cancer cells, as evidenced by laboratory experiments on rat, mouse and human cells. Similar frequencies also affect calcium loss from the brain. In fact, it is thought that the main problem with power lines may be due to their influence altering calcium metabolism in the body. This is likely from the range of symptoms suffered.

It is not a good idea to live *and* work in an area that has a combination of radar and radio transmissions and power lines, especially if there is a lot of underground water and lines of geopathic stress, and particularly if there is already a history of depressive or allergic illness in your family.

Safety guides

In some parts of the USA rights of way have been introduced to safeguard people from the effects of electromagnetic radiation. In Texas, for example, there must be 100 ft between the edge of a property and a 100–110 kV line; 150 ft from a 220–230 kV line; and 250 ft from a 345 kV line. Even these distances may now be a little outdated, in that 250 metres (800 ft) is probably better for a 345 kV line.

The frequencies of power lines are very close to those of human brain waves and muscular activity, so it is unreasonable to assume that they have no effect on our health. However, it is very difficult to measure anything underneath power-lines as the electromagnetism affects all of the measuring equipment. Furthermore although measurements may be taken by pushing the measuring apparatus in on a long stick, this will merely result in the measurement of the unperturbed electromagnetic field, which is not necessarily the same as what you would be exposed to if you stood underneath. This is because of the electric field enhancement effect, described below.

ELECTRIC FIELD ENHANCEMENT EFFECT

When any object, including a living body, enters an electromagnetic field, the field folds over that object so that its strength may be several hundred times that of the unperturbed field, while underneath the object there would be a much reduced reading. As far as the human body is concerned, the head is the part most affected by such field enhancement.

Unfortunately, we can neither see nor feel this electromagnetic radiation, just as we cannot see or feel X-rays, but this does not mean that it is not having any effect on us. Many of our deeper tissues are not sensitive to heat or touch; they do not need to be as they do not normally come into contact with either. Similarly, our bodies are not used to being exposed to the sort of electromagnetic radiation generated by power lines, as such radiation has only been with us for 50 years or so – a very short period of man's history.

We do know that ionisation is abnormal beneath power

lines, there being a predominance of positive ions, and we know that there are electric and magnetic fields. We also know that the electromagnetic field can be powerful enough to generate a current that can illuminate a fluorescent tube when this is placed underneath; an electric field of around 2.8 kV/m is all that is needed to give a faint light, while readings in an unperturbed field beneath power lines are often as high as 4–12 kV/m, depending on the capacity and load of the line.

Furthermore, a 400-kV power-line, fully loaded, would create an electromagnetic field for 250 metres on either side of the line, which could in turn generate electric currents in a living body comparable to those that give pain relief. This effect is possibly due to the body's release of endorphins in the brain – opiate-like chemicals responsible for pain relief and feelings of well-being. It is also possible, if you were continually exposed to this effect, that you could develop a dependency on your own natural drugs; it has been noticed by some farmers that their cows become 'junkies', preferring to stand under power pylons to eating. It is then also possible, of course, after long-term exposure, to feel withdrawal symptoms when away from such stimulation.

MAGNETIC FIELDS

The electric field drops off quite quickly with distance from a power line, and its frequency is clear, being that of the power line itself. The magnetic field, however, fluctuates much more; it has 'contaminating' frequencies, and does not decrease as quickly as the electric field with distance. Furthermore, with increased distance, there is more likely to be a uniform distribution of magnetic field over the body. The magnetic field beneath a 400-kV supergrid power-line may be anything from about 1 microtesla when the current is around 100 A, to 10 microtesla if the load is greater, usual maxima being around 5000 A. These are rough guideline figures, as much depends on load, capacity, ground and weather conditions, as well as a whole variety of other variables.

It is probable that it is exposure to the unbalanced non-uniform magnetic fields that causes the increased risk of heart disease, cancer, depression and thyroid problems. It has been observed that people on the ground-floors, or near the incoming supply, of high-rise flats have an average magnetic field exposure of around 0.2–0.4 micro-tesla, and are more susceptible to these problems than those on the top floors, where the magnetic field may be much lower, around 0.015 microtesla.

Depressive feelings may occur with continual exposure to less than 0.1 microtesla. This amounts to normal exposure; electrical workers, however, may experience levels of up to 5 microtesla (50 times as large) and a few even more. Electrical workers would therefore probably be wise not to live near overhead or underground electricity cables. Balance is important, and it is better to limit exposure.

Sleeping within a strong magnetic field may also be potentially more damaging than walking around in the same field and passing in and out of it. If you live near cables, sleep in the rooms furthest away. Interestingly, research has also found that *E. coli* (one of our most common bacteria found in the gut) does not flourish in a 50 Hz frequency electromagnetic field either. Further-more, well-water beneath power-lines does not appear to have any bacteria in it. Indeed, magnetic fields were once investigated for sterilising water in space.

DOMESTIC APPLIANCES

It has been estimated that 80 per cent of our magnetic field exposure comes from overhead or underground elec-tric cables, the rest being due to domestic sources. The point to remember with most of our domestic appliances (TVs and computers being possible exceptions) is that they are only on for short periods of time and often only part of the body is exposed to their electromagnetic field; so, although the fields may be quite strong locally, the appliances do not, perhaps, have such a damaging effect.

Electric blankets, however, do cause the entire body to be exposed to electromagnetic fields for quite a few hours. Some research has shown seasonal increases (September to June) in miscarriages in women who use electrically heated beds, including water beds. The use of electric blankets is also thought to affect a woman's menstrual cycle, and may be a contributory factor in the incidence of hormone-related cancers such as breast cancer, due to the effect on melatonin production. On top of that, electrically heated beds have been linked to slower foetal development and learning problems in children, especially if the mother slept in such a bed whilst pregnant. More research is necessary here, but in view of the increasing numbers of slow learners and those with specific learning problems such as dyslexia, the possible problem should be resolved sooner rather than later. Meanwhile, pregnant women might be well advised to cuddle up to husbands or hot-water bottles, rather than increasing their electricity bill, just in case.

LIVING WITH ELECTROMAGNETISM

It is known that earthworms are disturbed by underground electricity cables and move out, so altering the structure of the soil; hens beneath power lines lay scrambled eggs in thin shells; bees seal up their hives and become aggressive; cows lose their appetites; and birds such as homing pigeons become disorientated. Man is therefore unlikely to be unaffected by electromagnetic radiation; he's just indecisive.

Thankfully, we are already starting to clean up our chemical pollution, although an awful lot still needs to be done. The message of this section is that we should also consider our electromagnetic pollution. We have to start somewhere, even though we do not know safe levels of electromagnetic radiation yet. There does appear to be a possible link with cancer (especially leukaemia) and with depression. Learning disorders are also a potential problem, as well as all those general complaints of not feeling as well as we could.

Do we really want our electrical comforts so much that we are prepared to take a risk with our health and life? Probably not, but maybe we can have our cake and eat it too, although to do that we must be sensible and plan ahead. We need electricity, but new routes, substations, transmission lines, etc., need to be thought about and sited well away from people's homes and work. Perhaps car parks, cemeteries and other such places of intermittent activity could be sited at the borderlines between areas high in human activity and areas high in electromagnetic radiation.

We do not know all the answers to the electromagnetic problem, but in the light of present evidence it would seem sensible to avoid over-exposure, wherever possible, and to take heed of the widest safety guidelines in future planning. After all, it costs a lot of time and money to install all of this equipment, and even more to move it all again. It will also cost a lot of unnecessary pain and suffering over the coming years if the research is right and we do nothing about it.

POLLUTION IN THE HOME

15
FUELS

The general air temperature in a home is usually kept at around 18–21°C (65–70°F). In practice, however, this will vary a lot; rooms upstairs will be warmer than those downstairs, because hot air rises and there may be isolated pools of radiant heat, created by sunlight or just in front of a fire. But whatever temperature we aim for, there is no doubt that, in our present climate, we need some form of heating for part of the year. Our lifestyle also means that we need to be able to heat water and to cook all the year round. The form of energy that we choose needs to be economic, and, for conservation and personal economy, needs to be efficient and clean. It is also very important, however, that it has to have minimal harmful effects on our health.

Obviously, there is no way that we can avoid all of the potential hazards to health, but it is as well to be aware of the possible problems with all of the different fuels and then to make a personal choice accordingly. For example, some individuals are very sensitive to fumes from oil or gas, whilst others are electrically sensitive.

Below are some of the problems that you may encounter and what you can do to minimise the effects.

PARAFFIN/KEROSENE HEATERS

These heaters are generally portable, and so have no vents to the outside; because of this they release all of their fumes into the house, into the air that you have to breathe. They are therefore not really to be advised at all, although will possibly be all right for temporary heating in a well-ventilated room, as long as no one in that room is sensitive to the fumes.

Additionally, they are an obvious fire hazard. They will burn dust, so creating extra smells and fumes. The fumes they produce are not only dangerous, but also potentially 'addictive'; some people love the smell of their paraffin stoves, yet these are often the same people who are sensitive to them and find that their aches and pains vanish a week after they have removed them from the house.

GAS AND OIL HEATING

Fumes from gas or oil boilers or cookers are recognised as some of the most serious pollutants in the home; if they get into the air within a house they can cause a range of problems, from the mild to the intolerable, depending on the sensitivity of the individual. Very badly affected people may have to have all gas or oil appliances removed, and most of us would benefit by adopting a few basic measures to help reduce the risks of the fumes damaging our health.

- Try to locate the boiler for hot water or central heating outside the house, in a vented boiler-room made of noncombustible materials (not the garage, as this would create a fire hazard). This is obviously an expensive option, however; if you do not wish to incur the cost, and are not badly affected, try to make sure that the room housing the boiler is always well ventilated, and stock it with spider plants.
- Spider plants effectively utilise carbon monoxide – one of the problem products of gas and oil boilers. They also (as do other plants) increase the oxygen content of the air during periods of daylight or artificial lighting.
- It is unfortunate that boilers are often sited in the kitchen, where people spend a lot of time; window-sill herbs and plants, as well as open windows, can help to minimise the build-up of undesirable fumes and smells.
- Boilers and pumps should be checked regularly, and any vents or flues inspected for signs of corrosion and blockage.
- Although ventilation is important if you use a gas

cooker, any appliance with a naked flame should not be situated next to a window or door where a curtain or teatowel could be blown across it and catch fire.

- All kitchen cookers should be vented to the outside to remove undesirable gases and smells. Gas cookers, in particular, need extensive ventilation as they give off a lot of carbon monoxide and carbon dioxide, as well as nitrogen dioxide.
- Food spilled on the top of a cooker or in the oven can cause a considerable amount of air pollution, for if it is subsequently burned (probably whilst you are cooking something else), gases like carbon monoxide and benzopyrenes, as well as others, are produced.
- Stale or dirty kitchens are a health hazard in many ways, not just because of the risk of food poisoning.

ELECTRIC HEATING

Electric cookers and central heating are generally thought to be the healthiest option for most people, although it often isn't the cheapest or most convenient. However, if anyone in your family suffers from medical or allergy problems, electricity is well worth investigating.

Portable electric fires of the convection or radiant type are not so healthy, though. They fry dust and flies, so causing extra smells and pollution; are a potential fire hazard; will make surfaces and objects around them very hot – especially dangerous for young children; and are usually expensive to run.

Dirty or poorly maintained appliances are still a source of pollution, as described under the previous heading.

SOLID FUEL HEATING

Coal and wood fires produce irritant gases as well as soot and other toxins. They also take up a lot of the oxygen from the surrounding air, which can cause a negative pressure.

If you use this type of heating, chimneys need to be

clean, effective and not cracked or leaking in any way; cracks allow entry of more of the products of combustion into the house. Lined chimneys are best, as leakage of gases does occur through the bricks of unlined ones. In former days, chimneys were lined with a mixture of lime, mortar and cow dung, the resulting chemical reaction providing an effective impervious layer; not surprisingly, this method isn't used today.

Chimneys also have to be the required height above your house, so that smoke is distributed away from your living area. Unfortunately there is no legislation which dictates the height or siting of other people's chimneys in relation to your house, so it is wise to eye up next door's chimney when buying a house. Flats are often badly positioned from this point of view, and can be right in the 'smoke line' from other people's chimneys.

Boilers for solid fuel central heating are best situated in an outside boiler room, for the same reasons as for gas and oil boilers.

SOLAR HEATING

Solar heating is clean and nearly free to run. It is a system much used in other countries, but not so much here yet.

16
AIR POLLUTANTS

Burning anything consumes vital oxygen and replaces it with asphyxiating, carcinogenic or otherwise undesirable gases. This chapter will consider the main problems associated with the changes in our air caused by pollution in the home, both from combustion and other sources.

LOW OXYGEN LEVELS

Economy and energy conservation often lead us into creating what is virtually a sealed-home environment. However, excluding every draught and air flow has its problems, especially if a heating fuel or cooker is allowed to burn in such a restricted atmosphere.

The air we breathe in contains nearly 21 per cent oxygen. The body takes up some of this oxygen, so that the air we breathe out contains around 15.5 per cent oxygen. If we inhale air that contains less than 10 per cent oxygen the body becomes weak whilst the mind becomes euphoric, the combination obviously decreasing our chances of doing anything to rectify the situation. A good test to make sure that the oxygen level doesn't get that low is to light a candle, as this will be extinguished naturally when the oxygen content falls below 17 per cent. Fires consume oxygen as they burn; burning fires in an enclosed atmosphere therefore can create low oxygen levels.

PRODUCTS OF COMBUSTION

It is important to note that it is better to add fuel to a fire whilst it is still hot and red, for at high temperatures the gases produced as a result of burning fuel are ignited as they are liberated, so causing less problems. If the fire is allowed to die down before fuel is added, the liberation of these unburned noxious gases is increased.

Carbon monoxide

Carbon monoxide is the most abundant pollutant released during combustion, its concentration decreasing rapidly with distance from the fire or other fuel flame. It has an affinity for the haemoglobin in our blood which is responsible for taking up oxygen from the lungs and transporting it around the body. Once combined with the haemoglobin, the carbon monoxide blocks the uptake of oxygen; the body, and more importantly the brain, then become starved of oxygen. Carbon monoxide is therefore an asphyxiant, causing drowsiness and headaches in low concentrations and death in high doses. People who already have blood, circulatory, heart and lung diseases are particularly sensitive to it.

Carbon monoxide is given off from any burning gas, oil, paraffin, solid fuel or cigarette. It is also produced by cars; it is therefore preferable not to have the garage underneath any rooms of the house, as carbon monoxide and other fumes from car exhausts can easily pass up into the living area.

Indoor air can be expected to have levels above 0.5 parts per million (ppm) carbon monoxide, but levels of 100 ppm can easily be reached in a closed kitchen with a central heating boiler and cooker in use. This higher level of exposure should only be for short periods of time, and may well cause tiredness, headaches, dizziness and even nausea. Continued exposure over the years will result in loss of concentration and reduction in lung capacity and memory. Smokers are more susceptible to the effects of carbon monoxide, as they already have elevated blood levels of the gas.

Carbon dioxide

We tend to think of carbon dioxide as a good gas which in many ways, it is; its presence stimulates our need to breathe, and plants use it to make their food. But like anything else taken in excess, carbon dioxide can be harmful.

If the air contains 5 per cent carbon dioxide, breathing becomes laboured; at 8 per cent the lungs become congested; and levels of between 7 and 10 per cent are soon fatal. Even in modest doses it reduces concentration, alertness and the ability to make decisions. Fortunately, however, it is quite easy to detect an excess of carbon dioxide in the atmosphere, as you soon feel claustrophobic, and feel the need to get out of the stuffy atmosphere.

Nitrogen oxides

The principal source of the nitrogen oxides is the combustion of coal, oil, natural gas and petrol; wood burning will also cause their production, but is not a major source. Motor vehicles produce nitrogen oxides in their exhaust gases. During the daytime the action of ultraviolet light from the sun tends to convert the nitrogen oxide into nitrogen dioxide, but during the night the nitrogen oxide tends to predominate. Our indoor environment is also likely to contain high levels of nitrogen oxides, particularly if we have a boiler in the house, no cooker extractor fan, if we smoke or if we have a garage attached to the house.

Nitrogen oxides irritate any mucous tissue, and prolonged exposure can cause lung and respiratory damage. Nitrogen oxides also depress the immune system, in that they reduce the number and activity of the white blood cells. If working in your kitchen gives you watery eyes or a sore throat, and you easily succumb to coughs and colds, you could be getting too many nitrogen oxides. Check your heating and cooking systems.

Sulphur dioxide

Sulphur dioxide is more of a problem with solid fuel and oil central heating; natural gas combustion produces very little in comparison. In the kitchen, sulphur dioxide levels are not usually a problem for most people, although those with allergies or respiratory problems are more likely to be affected. Natural-fibre curtains and rugs will absorb sulphur dioxide to some extent, so if you do have an oil or solid-fuel system you will find that such fabrics need washing a lot and will tend to wear quite quickly due to the acid action of the sulphur dioxide.

OZONE

Ozone is produced by the action of sunlight on motor vehicle exhaust fumes. In the home ozone is made by the action of an electrical discharge on oxygen; most electrical equipment produces some ozone. The old ionisers designed to produce negative ions also produced ozone as a byproduct, and so overall, were not really beneficial.

Like the nitrogen oxides, ozone causes irritation of the eyes, nose, throat and lungs, and is more likely to affect anyone who already has a respiratory condition, including the allergic problems like hay fever and asthma. Ozone is responsible for the familiar smell when electrical devices are used; unfortunately many people have a decreased sense of smell (sometimes merely due to a simple nutrient deficiency, such as zinc or beta-carotene) which they may not be aware of and so cannot detect very low levels of ozone. And, like anything else, some people are more sensitive to ozone than others.

HUMIDITY

The type of heating system that we have will affect the humidity of the atmosphere in the house. All air contains some water vapour, depending on climate and weather conditions. We do, however, alter the humidity indoors, by:
- Breathing in an enclosed atmosphere.
- Sweating.
- Keeping plants.
- Doing the washing, especially if we have to dry clothes indoors.
- Having a shower or bath.
- Cooking.

- Heating.
- Insulation, or lack of it, and ventilation will also have an effect.

The more humid the atmosphere, the hotter it feels, so that 18–21°C (65–70°F) will appear quite comfortably warm if the air contains a good amount of water vapour. Conversely, if there is not enough water vapour, this sort of temperature will not feel so warm or comfortable, and you may be tempted to turn the heating up higher.

It is worth noting that hot, dry air dries out the skin and mucous linings, so causing faster aging, dry skin and increased likelihood of respiratory infections. Humidity is therefore very important for anyone with respiratory problems. It is also important for anyone with a cold or the flu; if you are bunged up you can often breathe better in a hot steaming bath, for example, or with your head over a bowl of steaming water. On the other hand you do not want so much humidity that nothing ever appears to be dry, condensation is constant, moulds grow on walls, and the air feels oppressive. It is important to get the balance right.

We are most comfortable when the air contains half its full capacity for holding water vapour. i.e. when its relative humidity is around 50 per cent. House plants will be happy with this, although they benefit from the occasional holiday in the bathroom. However, if your plants are always drying out then the relative humidity is probably too low. There are thermometers available, intended to measure relative humidity (one wet bulb and one dry), but they are rarely used or needed in the home.

In Britain we rarely need complicated devices to control humidity. However, it is a good idea to place a dish of water to evaporate near the fire or other source of heat, so keeping the air moist – as long as the water is changed daily so that it doesn't grow bacteria. Temperature controls should normally be set below 25°C (75°F), although bearing in mind that people with some medical conditions, e.g. cancer, do feel the cold much more than healthy individuals.

The problem with condensation

Too much humidity is best tackled naturally, if possible by opening windows and doors. If this is not possible fans are useful and, as a last resort, air conditioning can be introduced.

In this country cold air outside the house makes walls, windows and some ceilings cold. When warm indoor air carrying water vapour comes into contact with these cold surfaces, its temperature is lowered, reducing its ability to hold moisture, and the excess moisture is deposited on the cold surface. If the surface is wood, it will absorb this moisture and will eventually rot; other surfaces may grow bacteria and moulds, so causing health problems. The problems are not always apparent, e.g. moulds may grow in unseen places like lofts, and the spores released by the moulds can drop into the living area and then cause health problems.

The best, but costly, way to deal with this problem is to install double glazing and wall and loft insulation to reduce the cooling effect of the external environment, but the choice of material is important, as we shall see later.

THE NECESSITY FOR VENTILATION

Whatever home we live in we will have a contamination load, i.e. unwanted substances produced as a result of cooking, cleaning, breathing and doing our various hobbies. The materials that have been used to construct that home, and those that we bring into it, are all contributory factors to home pollution. It is therefore important to open windows and doors after we have finished painting or any other internal decorating.

With the increase in insulation, double glazing and draught-proofing in order to conserve fuel, there has to be thought given to how to remove these contaminants. For most of us in this climate, opening windows and fitting boilers, cookers, etc., with extractors is enough, but some environmentally sensitive people need to do more. People living on a very busy street, or near a chemical plant, a factory, or similar, may find that the outdoor air is worse than that inside and may prefer not to open their windows. All of these homes will therefore need other forms of ventilation to prevent the contaminants building up and affecting health. Indeed, fan systems or even filters may be required.

17
MATERIALS

The homes that we live in give us shelter from the elements, but sometimes they add hazards of their own. How safe are the materials with which we construct our homes? Can we improve these in any way? What materials should be avoided? How do our furnishings, carpets, curtains, etc., affect our mood, behaviour and health?

EFFECTS OF MATERIALS

Formaldehyde

Formaldehyde is a very common indoor contaminant. It is partly formaldehyde that gives a house that characteristic smell when you come back from holiday after having the house closed up for a week or two. In the laboratory it is excellent for preserving dead things – laboratory rats and the like. However the living should be very wary of this strong preservative, unless they too wish to become a human 'pickled onion'.

Formaldehyde is an irritant, affecting the eyes, throat, nose and lungs; in excess it causes runny eyes, sneezing, coughing, rapid pulse, weakness, headaches, indigestion-type pains and skin reactions. At lower concentration it can also be responsible for loss of sleep and depression, if encountered regularly. It has been shown to aggravate other illnesses, and possibly to sensitise individuals so that they become prone to allergies; in this respect it appears to be a kind of trigger.

Around half of the total aldehyde count in fog and polluted air is formaldehyde. Yet we eat this same chemical; we drink it in soft drinks and beer; we wear it; we spray it, read it and decorate with it. Around food it's used as an insecticide spray to kill flies and other insects. It is used in the synthesis of artificial vitamin A. It makes clothes wrinkle-proof, dye-fast, shrink-resistant, water-repellant, flame-resistant and more elastic. It is used in the tanning industry. We paint its resin on to our finger-nails, and spray it over ourselves in the form of deodorants and anti-perspirants. We gargle with it, wash in it, shampoo and set our hair in it. It's used in fabric dyes, paints, paint strippers, plaster, chipboard, wood preserva-tives and even concrete. Paper and photographs are strengthened by it. It's in nitrogen fertilisers, and in many disinfectants found in hospitals, bakeries and breweries (it is very effective against yeasts and moulds in particular). Diesel fumes are another common source; it is formalde-hyde that gives diesel fumes their familiar smell. You have to admit it's very useful stuff, but are we getting too much of it?

The harmful nature of formaldehyde in building and furnishing materials was brought to light in the 1970s when urea formaldehyde foam was sprayed into the walls of many houses to insulate them. After a few years so many people had experienced health problems due to it that it was banned from use in this way. As we have seen though, there are many less potent sources of this chem-ical, so it's worth trying to keep your exposure level down.

A major problem with formaldehyde is that it attaches itself to particles in the air, which are then breathed into the lungs where they cause inflammation. Ventilation is therefore very important if there are a lot of materials giving off formaldehyde in your home. The ever-useful spider plants will remove small quantities from the air, but even they are not too keen on the stuff; it apparently takes about 10 plants to keep a small room low in carbon monoxide and formaldehyde. (This is obviously a rough guide, as it depends on the degree of contamination and ventilation.)

Asbestos

Asbestos is a very inexpensive mineral fibre, once used extensively in buildings. In fact it is not a single substance, but a name for a variety of fibrous, mineral silicates found in nature; there are white varieties (chrysotile), blue ones (crocidolite) and brown ones (amosite). The fibres are resistant to heat, friction and acid; in addition, asbestos is flexible and has great tensile strength. Its main advantage in the construction industry is therefore its resistance to fire, and so it was used wherever fireproofing was advisable, especially in plaster, ceilings, ceiling tiles, insulation and even clothing. Asbestos cement, for example is to be preferred to ordinary cement when the made-up concrete has to withstand weathering. It has also been used in water-pipes and other pipe work, air conditioning ducts, corrugated roofing and garden furniture. It may be found in wicks for oil stoves and as an ingredient of some talcs.

Unfortunately, when the fibres become worn and form dust, asbestos particles are released and can be inhaled. Accumulation of these particles in the lungs causes scavenger cells (phagocytes) to be mobilised. These cells in turn release a biochemical called haemosiderin, and the iron from this substance coats the asbestos particles, in an attempt to protect the lung tissue. These coloured particles are found in the lungs of asbestos workers, where after 20 years or so of accumulation, these particles build up to a level where they cause thickening and calcification of the lung and even cancer or asbestosis.

Most of us have traces of asbestos in the lungs which probably originate from inhalation of motor vehicle emissions (brake pads and linings contain it) or burning wood, paper or coal. Now that we know its hazards we should try to avoid it and only employ experts with the correct equipment to dispose of it.

Plasticisers
Plasticisers are significant environmental pollutants.

Phthalates are plasticisers that give PVC its flexibility, PVC being used extensively in various appliances, upholstery and wall coverings, construction materials, medical equipment, food packaging and as a constituent of some cosmetics, perfumes and insect repellants. Plasticers get into sewage sludge, are ingested by fish, and have thus entered the human food chain. The subtle effects that this may have on humans is at present unknown, but work on fish has shown that it causes interference with calcium metabolism resulting in low blood-calcium levels.

PCBs can also be used as plasticisers, as well as solvents, adhesives and sealants. They degrade very slowly and are stored in the fatty tissue of animals, including humans. They get into the food chain, again via sewage and hence through fish, as well as by leaching into food from food packaging materials; the latter can be minimised by avoiding foods packaged in plastic, or by buying well in date and transferring to glass or other containers at home. There are many symptoms associated with accidental PCB excess; the after-effects certainly seem to involve disturbances to the central nervous system, but the effects of a daily low-level intake are not really known.

Flame-retardant chemicals

PBBs (polybrominated bi-phenyls) are closely related to PCBs. They are used as flame retardant chemicals, in which guise they are found on clothing. They are also eliminated very slowly from the body, and are stored in the fat. Sensitive individuals exposed to them may exhibit fatigue, headaches, joint and muscular pains, nausea and loss of appetite.

Other flame retardant chemicals may also be a problem, the most widely used of which is tris [2,3]-dibromopropyl phosphate, or tris-BP for short. It is put on to polyesters, in particular, in levels of up to 10 per cent of the fabric's weight. Unfortunately, tris-BP is taken up through the skin, and there is particular concern about its use in babies' and children's clothes; for example, a 200g pair of child's pyjamas could contain as much as 6g of this chemical, although it is fortunately washed out to a considerable degree. It is probably wise, therefore, to wash thoroughly, four or five times, any new garment or cover which is to be next to the skin before using it; this will remove many chemicals and dressings, whilst not reducing the flame retardant properties.

THPC, tetrakis-[hydroxy-methyl]-phosphonium chloride, is another flame-retardant chemical, releasing formaldehyde.

Because there is a 20–30 year time lag in the effect of this sort of chemical on the human body, and, of course, there are interactions with other chemicals during this time, it is difficult to evaluate their effects on human health at present. We have many new chemicals at our disposal, of which we know little about their effects either on us or on the environment; it is therefore wise to be cautious with their use.

Polyurethane
Polyurethanes are a group of chemicals found in upholstery materials; packaging materials; insulation and refrigeration materials; paints and varnishes; and soft toys.

Toluene diisocyanate, TDI, is the most significant chemical in this group from the health point of view. It is a fire hazard, and when it is burned it releases very toxic gases. Furthermore, instant polyurethane kits that are sometimes available for household use may give off fumes exceeding those permitted in any factory, so care and adequate ventilation is necessary during their use.

Immediate effects associated with polyurethane fumes, and noted particularly by firemen, are tightness of the chest, breathlessness, vomiting and poor balance. Inability to concentrate, memory loss, headaches and asthma-type problems are among the delayed symptoms.

PVCs
Polyvinyl chlorides can cause respiratory problems when heated. People wrapping foods with PVC film often cut it using a hot wire, and have been known to develop a sort of asthma; this is caused by the decomposition fumes, and disappears with withdrawal from exposure.

Timber-treatment chemicals
Lindane and pentachlorophenol are used in some timber

treatments, but are very toxic. Both are nerve poisons, can be absorbed via the skin and, like all the toxic organochlorines, are stored in the fat cells. However, the effects of these chemicals may not be noticed for years.

If you do get any of these chemicals on the skin, it would be wise to remove them as soon as possible, not to wait until you have finished the job. Protective clothing to prevent contamination would be better still.

INSULATION MATERIALS

The outside walls of our houses are bound to get wet, and once upon a time this meant that inside walls became damp too. Nowadays, though, we have two layers of brick (or blockwork), with a gap in between. If the ties holding these two layers together slope towards the outside, so preventing water from trickling down the ties into the inside wall, and there is no water-carrying material above the damp-proof course, the inside walls remain dry. Insulation can then be added or injected between the walls to help keep the heat in and any damp out, so our homes are snug and warm. The choice of such insulation materials is important, however, as any gas given off from them will seep into the house.

A few years ago, when cavity wall and roof insulation became very fashionable as a means of keeping homes warm and conserving fuel, urea formaldehyde foam was used as an insulation material. Subsequently, however, it was found to be a major source of formaldehyde contamination, causing various health problems, so it has now been banned for use in homes. Nevertheless, this underlines the need to know what has been used in the house that you spend so much of your time in; it makes it easier to spot materials that might be affecting your health if you know what has been used and what their effects might be.

Plastic resins like polystyrene balls and polyurethane are now more likely to be the material of choice when putting in cavity wall insulation. Other insulating materials are glass, mineral or cellulose fibres, these all being used in roof spaces to prevent your hard-earned heat from escaping to warm up the sky. This latter group is usually fine, the main problem being that the fibres do give off a dust to which some people react, although this can usually be minimised. Sometimes the fibres contain fire-retardant chemicals which can, again, cause irritation for some people. If you are thinking of having roof insulation put in and you tend to be chemically sensitive, it might be a good idea to live with a piece of the chosen material in fairly close proximity to make sure that it doesn't affect you, before paying to have the whole roof space covered.

Expanded mineral slag such as vermiculite is also an effective insulating material, especially for flat roofs. This material is rather like natural polystyrene balls; it is made of natural minerals, is light and bulky, and doesn't really carry any potential health hazard apart from dust.

OTHER BUILDING MATERIALS

Concrete

Concrete is usually a good material to use. It is one of the least permeable to radon gas, so is very useful for floors, in particular in areas where this naturally occurring contaminant may be high.

Sometimes, however, additives such as detergents, petrol-based chemicals and formaldehyde are used in concrete. If you are having concrete laid it is therefore a good idea to enquire about the additives before the work is done.

Brick, blocks and stone

Brick, concrete blocks and stone are also materials that rarely cause sensitivity problems, although stone is more permeable to both radon and water than is concrete.

Decorative imitation (plastic) bricks can cause problems, however.

Wood and board

Wood is a lovely natural material, but there are some potential problems to consider.

For example, a few people are very sensitive to the fumes given out by pine, will feel ill in houses with pine cladding or pine furniture, and will probably even be sensitive to the smell of pine forests or pine trees in the garden. Tree resins in all softwoods (cedar, fir, spruce, pine) can cause irritation, and are best well sealed with an additive-free lacquer sealant. Hardwoods cause less sensitivity problems.

Some wood preservatives, however, do contain unpleasant chemicals which continue to be given off some time after application. Glues, too, are often a potent source of formaldehyde, and should be used with care; chipboard, for example, contains a lot of formaldehyde glue and is best avoided whenever possible.

Waterproof materials
Glass and metals like steel and aluminium do not pose health problems when used in construction, but asphalt, tar, some plastics and rubber all release undesirable chemicals, especially when heated, and are not advised for confined areas.

SOFT FURNISHING MATERIALS

Apart from the materials that are used to construct your home, there are also those that are used to make it comfortable inside. There has been quite a lot of concern shown about making soft furnishings less of a fire hazard, beds and chairs better for your back, and taking the lead out of paint, but what generally are the best or the worst materials with which to furnish your home, and why?

As you read this section, remember that everyone has their own specific sensitivities and that it is up to each individual or family to consider the information and to decide which materials to avoid and those which may not be a problem to them.

Carpets
Natural fibres like cotton or wool are well tolerated by

most people, although some individuals do have a contact sensitivity for wool and so cannot wear woollen jumpers, etc. If you are sensitive to wool, a cotton, acetate or rayon fibre may be preferable if you often lie on the floor with your skin in contact with the carpet. Most wool sensitives can tolerate a wool carpet, however, although a crawling infant with eczema may well be reacting to this type of carpet.

Some chemical additives, such as dyes, moth-proofing and fire-retarding chemicals, can cause problems on natural-fibre carpets. It is useful if you are able to take away a square of any carpet that you are proposing to buy to make sure that you are not sensitive to it before you purchase the lot.

Synthetic carpets made out of nylon or polypropylene give off gases such as benzene, formaldehyde, toluene and xylene. The rayons and acetates are better in this respect as they are based on cellulose (a natural fibre) and so do not give off these gases. Foam-rubber or plastic-type backings to carpets do give off gases for some time after they have been laid, as do linoleum and the soft plastic floor-tiles.

Fabrics

Those fabrics used for curtains, furniture and covers may give off gases, too, especially if they are exposed to sunlight or other forms of direct heat. Again, from the contamination point of view, cotton, rayon, acetate and possibly wool, as well as silk, linen and jute, are to be preferred to polyesters and nylons.

All these fabrics are often treated with chemicals to make them crease resistant, flame proof, moth resistant, stain resistant, etc. Whilst being very convenient, these chemical treatments do cause problems for allergic individuals.

Leather is not such a good natural material, as the odours from the tanning process may contain formaldehyde. The plastic imitation alternatives to leather are even worse from this point of view.

Plastics

Vinyl mattress-covers should not be used at all, especially for babies. Not only are they uncomfortable and 'sweaty', but they give off gases for a long time, and if inhaled these may reduce the desire to breathe. Babies should definitely not lie on plastic mattress covers (or plastic playmats, nappy changers, etc.) for any prolonged period of time, and preferably not at all.

Another disaster area for the allergic child is the bean bag – you don't have to get near one to smell the gases coming off, even years after it has been purchased. Furniture containing fillers such as sytrene-foam chips, polyurethane foams or foamed rubber should be avoided wherever possible.

Feathers

Feathers are one of the softest fillers for pillows, but many people dare not bury their nose in a feather pillow for fear they will start sneezing or suffer some other allergic reaction. Even for those of us who are fortunate enough not to react in this way, it is a wise precaution to use a cotton barrier cloth (one that is very closely woven, allowing the passage of air and moisture, but not feathers) or several old pillowcases beneath the top one so that the feathers can't escape and cause problems.

Down and hair should be treated with the same care.

OTHER MATERIALS USED IN THE HOME

The kitchen will dominate this section, as this is where we use the most materials.

Furniture

Furniture in the kitchen is much more likely to be exposed to fluctuating temperatures and humidity than furniture anywhere else in the house, which in turn will cause greater release of gases like formaldehyde, present in chipboards in particular.

Old cupboards may be less of a problem, having given

off most of their load in previous years; and there is a new, low-emission type of chipboard which gives off less in the way of contaminants. New ordinary particle-board type cupboards are going to smell the most, unless sealed internally and externally with a sealant, waterproof paint, varnish or plastic veneer. Metal or solid wood units are obviously less contaminating, but are more expensive.

Hard vinyl flooring
This is made from very stable plastic and doesn't usually cause any problems. However soft plastic or cushion-type flooring, as well as chemically-treated stain-resistant type kitchen carpet, often gives off fumes for some months or even years after laying.

Tiles
Tiles do not give off any gases and are easy to clean, so they are very good for kitchen floors and walls. However they are often used on work surfaces, and here they are not so good, for if food is put on to them or pastry is rolled out on them, the cracks in between tiles collect food, dirt, cleaning fluids, etc. This encourages bacterial growth, which isn't really desirable from the point of view of hygiene. Soft-woods are also unsuitable for work surfaces as moisture soaks in, causing fungal growth – again bad for hygiene and liable to rot the wood. Hard-woods, hard plastic laminate or marble are probably the best for work surfaces.

Wooden utensils
Wooden spoons, chopping boards, etc., should be dried out in a warm oven after washing – an oven, turned off after baking, will usually suffice. If they are merely washed up, dried with a cloth and put away they will grow a thin film of mould before the next baking day, which will end up in the food.

Pots and pans
Glass or stainless steel pans are the best to use with your

good health in mind, although from a practical point of view glass is not so good for milk and custard, as the glass holds the heat after you have turned the cooker off and the milk then tends to boil over. There is no contamination from glass dishes and pans, however.

Copper and iron saucepans may dissolve a little into the food, but they are not as bad as the aluminium or non-stick pans. Aluminium is very reactive; acidic foods like fruits, in particular, will readily dissolve aluminium into the food. Jam making in aluminium pans is one of the worst offenders. Non-stick Teflon (polytetrafluorethylene) pans sometimes give off fumes when used at high temperatures, and pieces of the coating can flake off into the food.

It is also worth noting that some foods, especially damp or acidic ones, will take up aluminium from aluminium-foil wrapping. This should only be used for very short storage periods, if at all.

Plastics

Plastic is very versatile stuff, but it does have its drawbacks and we should be aware of these so that we use the right plastic for the job.

One very important point to remember is that not all plastics are suitable for use with food; for example, the coloured plastic bucket made for general utility use is not suitable for fermenting beer in. Not all plastic containers are suitable for yoghurt or food storage; the plasticisers and colourants may pass into the food if the plastic is not of a food grade. So only use food-grade plastic containers for food and drink, and certainly don't heat or cook in plastic containers that were not manufactured for the purpose.

Do not leave food in plastic bags, etc., for longer than is necessary. Cheeses, for example, may be wrapped in plastic for clean and convenient transport home, but should then be transferred into a glass container before storing in the fridge.

For use in microwave ovens, Pyrex dishes are better than the cheaper plastic dishes sometimes given free with, or purchased for use in, these appliances. It is also better to use damp towels rather than the often suggested plastic-film cover when microwaving, as plasticisers used in the manufacture of this roll film have been shown to pass into the food, especially when it is heated. Fatty foods, in particular, take up more plasticiser than other foods. Such plastic clear-film is therefore best avoided altogether, or used only for carrying and protecting food from flies, etc., for short periods of time. (There is a plasticiser-free film available from Food Watch, but it is not suitable for use in microwaves.)

Paper

On average each of us uses two whole trees a year as paper. This doesn't usually cause any allergy problems, although some people are sensitive to the inks used in printing. However stored paper can be a problem if it is alowed to become damp as it will grow mould; and newspaper used as carpet underlay should be changed regularly if it is liable to get damp.

Many paper products are bleached with chlorine, and this can cause the formation of dioxin, which is extremely toxic. It is therefore not a good idea to wrap food in 'unknown' paper, for if dioxin is present it can pass into the food, especially if the food has a fat content; milk cartons are notorious in this respect. Dioxins have even been found in coffee passed through bleached filters and in other foods wrapped in bleached paper. Some countries like New Zealand now ban bleaching of paper in this way for food wrap. There is also some concern that dioxins could pass through the skin, allowing products such as toilet rolls, sanitary towels, etc., to be possible sources of irritation as well as contamination.

There are now, thankfully, non-chlorine bleached products available. If bleached white paper is liable to contaminate our food, then let's make it quite clear that we prefer our packaging to be less white.

18
DOMESTIC CHEMICAL POLLUTION

Hundreds of chemicals are used every year in our attempts to clean, repair, maintain and beautify our homes. These chemicals were obviously thought to be safe when they were introduced, but experience has shown that many have undesirable side effects.

The main aim of any chemical that we might use is to do the job that we want it to do, whilst doing as little harm as possible, but one of the problems with chemicals is that their interactions may have unexpected results. Whilst a single chemical may have been tested and considered safe for use, it may not be safe when used with other chemicals. It is therefore a good idea to use as few chemicals as possible and not to mix them. If you do get any chemicals on the skin which were not intended for that purpose, wash them off as soon and as thoroughly as possible. If you do have to inhale any fumes, restrict inhalation and get some fresh air as soon afterwards as you can.

All chemicals, even cosmetics, should be safely stored out of range of young children and pets; it has been known for small children to drink things like nail-varnish remover, for example. All chemicals should be stored with their tops firmly on so that solvents, etc., cannot escape into the air or leak and contaminate other things. Even things like soap should not be carried or stored next to foodstuffs, or the smell will taint the food.

PESTICIDES IN THE HOME

For centuries man has been at war with insects and other pests – flies, wasps, beetles, bugs, moths and cockroaches. Then came the introduction of DDT in the 1930s, the advent of pesticide sprays and the development of many other chemicals designed to destroy these pests.

Unfortunately, insects are very resilient and adaptable, so that nowadays many have developed resistance to these chemicals. A more serious problem was the discovery that the chemicals could easily get into the food chain, with all sorts of unforeseen consequences. These penetrating, cumulative and long-lasting poisons are still contaminating our environment, causing undesirable effects on man – destroying enzymes, blocking energy production processes and probably causing cancer – despite the fact that many of the chemicals have now been banned. When they get into the food chain, the poisons are not always broken down. They pass up the chain and are usually deposited in fatty tissues, which means that we are liable to get a greater dose if we eat a lot of animal fat. The chemicals are then stored in our own fatty tissues, to be released into our bodies if we go on a diet to lose those extra pounds. Obviously, everyone is different and will have his or her own tolerance level for these chemicals, a lot being dependent on the state of health and the total amount of pollutants to which they are exposed.

There was a time when electric vaporisers were fashionable, spreading lindane around hospitals, shops, schools, etc., and contamining everyone and everything, including food, with this very poisonous chemical. Another fashion was to treat woollens with dieldrin to make them moth-proof, even though this chemical can be absorbed through the skin.

The organochlorines and organophosphates are therefore to be treated as dangerous chemicals; it is better to avoid their use in the home if possible. There are alternative pesticides; they may not be quite as effective as the chemicals described above, but they are a lot safer. For example, pyrethrum flower (*Chrysanthemum cinerarii-folium*) is the source of the best known natural insecticide, pyrethrum powder, which used to be used in insecticides until the advent of more convenient substances. Now it is making a comeback as the main effective constituent of biofriendly insect repellent powders; it causes rapid paralysis of a wide range of insects but is completely non-toxic to mammals. Indeed pyrethrum and tansy (*Tanacetum bulgare*) have long been used to deter flies; one of the weekly household chores used to be to hang bunches of these flowers in kitchens for this purpose. The flowers themselves can also be grown in the kitchen, of course.

Clothing may be protected from moths by using the above flowers, along with lavender. All ground together and sewn into cloth bags, these moth repellants last for three to six months – the more pyrethrum, the longer it is effective.

Ants can be destroyed by using a mixture of icing sugar and borax. The ants take this back to their nest, where the borax destroys their boron balance and kills them. Cockroaches are similarly affected.

CHEMICALS IN THE KITCHEN

There are many many household chores to be done. It has been estimated that, averaged out, someone in every household has to spend more than 30 complete days a year cleaning. There are ways of doing this cleaning that are better for the environment and for your health while still being effective. So what are the problems, and what are the solutions?

Washing powder

One of the major environment-conscious changes recently has been to remove phosphates from washing powders and other household products, because of the problems that phosphates cause when they go down the drain and get into the waterways.

Washing powders also contain a lot of other chemicals.

There are surfactants, which are petroleum based; bleach to remove stains and prevent yellowing (these are better if they are chlorine free); preservatives to prevent the powder going mouldy; and whiteners. Biological powders may contain either bacteria or enzymes to digest and dissolve dirt, and these may sometimes cause dermatitis on the hands if they are not washed thoroughly after use, or may cause eczema on the body if the clothes are worn next to the skin and rinsing has been insufficient. Breathing in these washing powders causes more problems than skin contact, as the lung tissue is much more sensitive.

Pure unscented soap which has not been bleached may be your only option if you are sensitive to any of the ordinary washing powders. Soap is basically an alkali and fatty acid mixture which is easily broken down by bacteria and so presents less problems for the environment than do the modern-day detergents. The addition of a tablespoonful of vinegar to a pint of water in the final rinse removes any traces of scum or soap, and leaves the washed clothes very slightly acidic, which is preferable for your skin. This, incidentally, is a treatment advised for nappies; babies do not get nappy rash if their nappies are changed when necessary and given a final vinegar-rinse when washed, for it is the ammonia formed from urine which is a major cause of nappy rash, and this is neutralised by the vinegar.

If your water is hard it will be very difficult to use plain soap unless the water is softened first, otherwise it just forms a scum. Water can be softened by adding a dessertspoonful of borax per gallon (4.5 litres) of water.

Soapwort (*Saponaria officinalis*) can be used as a cleaning agent for delicate fabrics.

Washing-up liquids

These have never contained phosphates, so a phosphate-free label on the bottle signifies nothing. However washing-up liquids do contain colours, perfumes and petroleum-based grease removers. Personally I do not wish to eat washing-up liquid, and so very rarely use it, and then only for really stubborn grease that sodium bicarbonate will not remove. Every now and then I use it for glasses, but always make sure that they are thoroughly rinsed. I also use it for glass vases, which of course are used neither for eating nor drinking from.

If you have a dishwasher but react to the detergent, you can use a very small amount of soap – only about half a teaspoon or it will foam too much – and three tablespoons of baking soda for ordinary, not heavily greased, dishes.

Glass cleaners
Window and glass furniture cleaners are essential, the trigger containers being better for the environment than the aerosols. However, white vinegar also works well, and has the advantages both of being cheaper and of acting as an antifungal agent, the latter being very useful if there are any condensation problems. About three or four table-spoonfuls of vinegar to the pint ($\frac{1}{2}$ litre) of water is about right; if the glass is cleaned often, less will do, and if it is really grubby you may need a little more.

Vinegar may also be used effectively to clean the bath and tiles. Non-chlorine bleach should be used in prefer-ence for cleaning the loo, and should not be used with other cleaners at the same time.

Furniture Polish
Polish should be used on wooden furniture and floors. Using beeswax supports beekeepers, and is environmen-tally preferable to artificial, spray-canned products. Mineral oil can also be used; this is left on the furniture or floor for a while and then dried off.

Scouring powders and pads
Some plants can be used for polishing or scouring. The large quantities of silica deposited in the stalks of the equisetums, or horsetails, make them especially good for this; *Equisetum hyemale* has been named the scouring rush or pewterwort because it will effectively clean pewter

and other saucepans, utensils and wooden surfaces.

Plants with a high acid content like rhubarb are also very effective cleaners of saucepans, etc., leaving shining clean pans after being boiled in them. Indeed, if strong rhubarb solution is left in an aluminium pan it may well be strong enough to burn a hole in the bottom. Rhubarb is best cooked in glass pans if it is to be eaten as it is strong enough to dissolve some of the metal from the pan, which will then go into the food.

If a pan has been used for milk, porridge, eggs, etc., and is difficult to clean, boiling some rhubarb, lemon or vinegar in it, then leaving it for a while, will loosen the congealed food, making it easier to remove.

Metal cleaning

- Silver can be cleaned by placing the item in an aluminium pan for a quarter of an hour, along with hot water, baking soda and a pinch of salt.
- Copper and brass may be brightened by rubbing with lemon juice and baking soda.
- Rust can be removed from iron and steel by soaking for a few hours in paraffin (preferably out of doors) and then rubbing with an abrasive cloth.

Odour removers

Baking soda is a good air freshener – in the fridge, or anywhere else where odours need to be removed. It is also good as a dry carpet-cleaner; sprinkle it on and leave it for a few hours before vacuuming, and it will remove smells, especially stale cigarette smoke.

Air fresheners are common now, but by using baking soda, good ventilation and herbal air sweeteners the more hazardous aerosols can be avoided. Traditionally, lavender and tansy were strewn around the floors to do this job; now these flowers, plus others like sandalwood and cedarwood, can be placed in bowls or in cloth bags and allowed to impart their aroma to the house. There are many other ready-prepared potpourris on the market.

DRY-CLEANING FLUIDS

These are notorious and very bad for you if inhaled. It has been known for drivers to be rendered momentarily unconscious by the fumes of these fluids when they were taking their laundry home from the cleaners in the car. Articles that have been dry cleaned should be hung for a while in order to remove the vapours.

Tar or bicycle oil may be removed by rubbing with eucalyptus oil before washing.

THE CAR

If you buy a new car it always smells 'new'. This odour is the combination of dozens of chemicals used to produce the car's pristine interior. The outgassing will continue for months, although probably only noticeably so for a few weeks. During this time it is therefore a good idea to leave the doors or windows open as much as possible, to allow these fumes to escape. This is sometimes difficult if you have to park in the street all the time, but if you have your own drive it should be possible to leave all the windows open at least some of the time.

Remember to use safety procedures when tackling car maintenance, ensuring not to breathe in more fumes than necessary, either from the car itself or from the cleaners, paints or repair chemicals used. Never suck petrol up through a tube; the fumes will go into your mouth, even if you stop sucking before the liquid does. If you are running the engine a lot in the garage, even with the doors open, you will breathe in more fumes than if the car is outside. Not only that; if the garage is an integral part of the house, the fumes will go up into the rooms above and accumulate there.

DIY

Paints and other volatile organic compounds

Paints can be potent irritants, which is why it is advised to avoid a newly painted room for anything from 5 to 30 days, depending on how sensitive you are; those who find that cosmetics, perfumes and cleaning chemicals give them problems will be the first to react. During both the painting and airing time, therefore, the room should be well ventilated; leave all the windows open when possible, and close the door to the rest of the house, so sealing off the smell and letting the vapours escape.

Paints and some glues and plastics contain volatile petroleum solvents which readily evaporate into the air, giving the characteristic smell. They are toxic to brain cells (and remember, we produce no more of these cells; what we are born with is all that we get, and if any are destroyed there are no replacements). Most of these volatile organic compounds are asphyxiants, i.e. they cause suffocation. If you are exposed to them for long periods of time, symptoms may include dizziness, disorientation, blurring of outlines and fuzziness. Some are also depressants, with obvious results, while others act on the nervous system causing muscle weakness and lethargy.

- Any materials containing aldehydes, alkanes, alkenes, benzenes, butane, ethers, ketones, naphthas, propane, toluene, and xylene may well induce the above reactions.
- Latex paints containing rubber and acrylics give off strong smells and contain a lot of additives to prevent mildew, colour loss, etc.
- Epoxy paints, varnishes and resins are probably the worst sort to get; they give off strong fumes for a considerable period of time.
- Organochlorines and the organic bromines and fluorines are mostly toxic, some being very toxic and carrying a cancer risk. They are sometimes found in paints, but are also found in pesticides (probably the most toxic compounds of all), cleaning fluids, plastics and waxes.

If you have to use any of these materials as part of your occupation, it is worth remembering that you will become accustomed to the smells and your body will try to adapt. However this does not mean that no damage is being done.

It is therefore far better to take precautions, wear a respiratory mask when necessary, and well ventilate the area you are working in. Do not work in an enclosed room and paint regardless.

If you are exposed to these sorts of materials while your office or place of work is being decorated, try to ventilate your area as often as possible and to take frequent breaks, outdoors or with your head out of the window. The worst time will probably be on a Monday morning, when the workplace has been shut up all weekend. If you find that you are getting any symptoms, or headaches, sore skin, sore eyes or sore throat, point the problem out to your employer and see how things can be improved. In the short term, vitamin C powder, stirred into water or fruit juice and sipped throughout the day, will help to alleviate the symptoms. You will probably need a gram or two above your normal intake to get any relief, but the necessary dose can only be arrived at through trial and error.

If you do tend to be chemically sensitive it is probably best to test a small area of the house, e.g. one wall in the smallest loo, with the paint you want to use, and live with it for a few weeks before painting larger areas. Most people tolerate most paints, but it is always best to shut off the room for a week or so after painting, and leave the windows open whenever possible to let the smell out. If you really have to use the room, decorate in the summer when you can open all the windows most of the time without being freezing cold or wasting your heat.

There are hypoallergenic paints available, based on milk protein – hence the name casein paint – which do not usually cause any problems. The old-fashioned whitewash (lime in water) is also quite safe.

Wallpapers
Wallpapers are often used for internal decoration, while foil paper can be used effectively to screen out some forms of radiation. The vinyl and ready-glued papers are not too good as they give off formaldehyde and vinyl into the air. Some wallpaper pastes also cause irritation, usually the

ones that contain fungicides. It is often trial and error finding suitable ones.

Adhesives
Paper glues may contain casein and acrylics, but don't usually contain petroleum solvents. They are therefore reasonably harmless, as are basic wallpaper glues, which are starch based. Those containing a lot of other chemicals such as mould retardants may cause more of a problem, while urea-based and plastic-resin glues are much more toxic and give off formaldehyde.

Some wall and floor tile adhesives contain solvents and should only be used when there is plenty of ventilation. However there are hypoallergenic alternatives available if you find yourself sensitive to the solvent based ones.

Carpet adhesives are more likely to be a problem, as the solvent gases can easily pass through the material of the carpet. The golden rules are probably to be guided by the smell, to limit your exposure time accordingly and to work with good ventilation. Getting used to the smell is not a good indicator that you can tolerate the chemical.

Treating wooden floors
Wooden floors can be a problem, in that they need sanding and then treating with preservatives and varnishes, or need waxing, all of which can cause health problems for the sensitive. So always ventilate well during and after undertaking any of these tasks.

19
GADGETS

We live in a world of labour-saving, useful (and useless), fun (and frustrating) gadgets. Life would not be the same without many of them; they are taken for granted as part of the daily routine. Yet they do cause chemical and/or electromagnetic contamination, as well as consuming precious energy; we need to know the possible problems in order to use our gadgets to our best advantage.

This chapter lists some of our favourite gadgets, details the problems they may cause and shows how to minimise them. It is not intended that the chapter should be read as an 'every gadget is bad for you' message; it is merely intended to help those who may be very environmentally sensitive to spot their problem areas, and for the rest of us to minimise our exposure to unnecessary pollution.

COOKERS

These are absolutely essential – there are very few people who eat only raw food. The main problems with cookers have been dealt with more fully in Chapter 15 on fuels. Basically, gas and solid fuel cookers are more likely to cause problems for the allergic individual than are electric ones. If you do have either of the former, the kitchen should be well ventilated to get rid of any gas leaks and products of combustion (spider plants will help to remove these to some degree). It is therefore preferable to have any cooker fitted with a hood and extractor fan to the outside.

Electric cookers may be a problem for a few very electromagnetically sensitive individuals, but are usually fine for most people; there is no problem with contaminating gases. However, as with any cooker, it should be kept clean, as burning food produces toxins of its own.

Microwave cookers

These do not produce chemical contamination of the air, and even an electrically sensitive person may tolerate food cooked in a microwave better than food cooked in any other way, as the frequency of the electromagnetic radiation is different. People with severe food allergies may also find that they can tolerate microwaved food better than that cooked conventionally. It is at least worth trying a microwave if you have a lot of problems with cooked food.

However there is the problem with possible radiation leaks. As we cannot detect such escapes with our ordinary senses, it is difficult for us to know whether there is a problem or not, especially as some of the simple so-called detectors on the market are ineffective.

Although the radiation from microwaves is non-ionising, it does produce thermal effects, so obviously should not be used on living things. Microwaved food is reported to have vitamin losses greater than from food cooked convention-ally, although it will probably retain more minerals and B vitamins. The main problem really is whether any micro-waves are getting out of the machine or not. Microwaves are known to cause cataracts and are thought to have a detrimental effect on the nervous and cardiovascular systems.

Other cooking pots

Steamers, slow cookers and pressure cookers are all good ways of cooking, producing few contaminants and retaining maximum nutrients. Stainless steel and glass pans are definitely much better to use than any of the others, particularly aluminium ones, from the health point of view.

HEATERS

These have also been dealt with in Chapter 15, on fuels. To summarise, though, gas, solid fuel and oil boilers should ideally be positioned outside of the main living area. Radiators are better than open fires; open heaters (electric, gas, paraffin or solid fuel) are more of a fire hazard and contaminate the air with products of combustion and fried dust. They also cause more concentrated heat in their vicinity, which in turn causes outgassing, especially of formaldehyde, from other materials close to them.

Even small electric table-top appliances can produce odours and gases, as well as electromagnetic radiation. From the safety and pollution standpoint, it is always a good idea to switch these heaters off at the wall-plug when they are not in use.

Hair dryers
These fry dust and hair, and also produce oily fumes and ozone, so they can be a particular bother to people with respiratory allergies or illnesses. It is important to store them so that dust cannot accumulate on the heating element.

Irons
These can, of course, produce fumes, depending on the age and chemical content of the fabrics ironed.

SMALL MOTOR GADGETS

Ozone can be produced by small motors, e.g. blenders, food processors, coffee mills, ionisers, etc., and this in turn can cause irritation for some people. Food processors and fridges also produce oil fumes which cannot be tolerated by some people. Ventilation is therefore important when such machines are in use, even toasters and grills.

Most of our gadgets that produce electromagnetic radiation are only in use for short periods of time and the exposure is not over the entire body, so it is not too great a problem.

WASHING MACHINES

These, too, produce oil and detergent odours. If such

odours cause you problems then the machine will have to be located in a utility room or in the garage. Alternatively try changing the washing powder or liquid, to make sure that it is not either of these that is causing you the problems.

FRIDGES

Fridges have motors and pumps that contaminate the air with oils and refrigerants; they therefore need adequate ventilation to the outside, and cooling, to be safe and effective. Glass- and metal-lined refrigerators are better than plastic-lined ones as the latter smell and can taint the food.

LIGHTING

Electric lights are now commonplace, yet 200 years ago we didn't even have gas or petrol lights, only firelight, candle-light and natural daylight. Electric lighting has only been around for about 100 years, and fluorescent lighting less than half of that time.

Turning conventional incandescent lights out when they are not needed makes health sense as well as economic sense, as these lights heat up a lot and may release odours and fry dust when they get too hot. Similarly, shades should ideally be made of glass; if they are made of plastic or fabric they are more likely to smell and cause fire problems. Always use the correct wattage bulb for the lampshade.

Fluorescent lighting costs less to run after initially switching it on as little electricity is used to keep it going. Fluorescent lights use a gas, usually mercury vapour, which heats up when an electric current is passed through it. The gas glows with a bluish-green light, so another chemical, phosphor, is usually added to make the light yellower. However, flourescent strip lights vibrate, make disturbing humming noises and can be very irritating to some people when in operation. They are also very harsh, and produce more electromagnetic radiation than do conventional incandescent lights; because of this fluorescent lamps should be at least 4 feet away from the body. They are reported to increase feelings of depression. Electronic devices which were used in old flourescent strip lamps to start them could contain PCBs which are very toxic, so it is worth throwing these old tubes away (although not where they could cause contamination).

ELECTRIC BLANKETS

The type of electric blanket that you leave on whilst sleeping may prove to be a particular hazard, especially to pregnant women and babies. Research is still underway, but the general feeling is that the electromagnetic radiation coming from these devices may cause miscarriages in some women and learning disorders in children. Evidence is not conclusive but is it worth taking the risk?

It is perhaps best to sleep in a room without any electrical devices such as blankets, clocks, radios, TVs or computers, as all these may alter or disturb sleep rhythms.

TV AND COMPUTER SCREENS

Computers are increasingly becoming part of the range of equipment in the home, but I shall cover their problems in the chapter on office equipment. Televisions, however, are found in almost every home – very few people would want to be without one. Electromagnetic radiation comes from all sides of a TV set, so it is not a good idea to sit close to the side or at the back of the set, and it is particularly unwise to sit too near a TV screen; some children, especially, seem to sit or lie right in front of it. Electromagnetic radiation drops off considerably with distance, so obviously has much less of an effect on the body if you are sitting further away. This is one of the problems with a computer, the fact that you have to sit right in front of the screen.

From both the financial and health point of view, it is advisable to switch a TV set off if no one is watching it.

WATER FILTERS

Water filters are becoming ever more common. In some areas, however, they are not needed, but in others they may be, so check with your local water authority first.

Conventional jug filters are all right as long as the filter is changed often. There is no obvious way of telling whether the filter is still doing its job properly or not, but you can assume that filters will not last long in hard water areas as they will quickly become clogged with calcium deposits. The main problem with these simple filters is that, if they are not kept clean and changed often, they can grow bacteria and then actually contaminate the water.

Reverse osmosis units are probably better in badly contaminated areas, although they are much more expensive to install.

CARS

The car is another almost essential machine for most people.

Ideally it should be stored away from the house itself. The worst position in which to have the garage is under or next to the main rooms of your house; fumes from the car can then drift into the rooms and cause pollution problems in an enclosed space. If your garage is in such a position it is best to work on the car outside, or at least open the windows of the rooms. When you park the car, leave the garage doors open until the car has cooled down, and close them later, allowing better dispersion of undesirable smells and gases.

20
COSMETICS

Each year we spend a fortune in both time and money on cosmetics. Throughout history, and across all nations, women, in particular, have painted their faces and adorned their bodies with paints and jewellery to make themselves more beautiful. Men too, use cosmetics – in western cultures not usually as much as women, but in some cultures, however, they use more.

Cosmetics should be used with care and with regard to long-time effects, as well as short-term appeal. It is known that some substances, in particular those which are fat soluble, can be absorbed through the skin. Remember the ladies of Elizabethan times who used lead-based paints on their faces to whiten their skins; many subsequently died of lead poisoning, without realising what it was that was damaging their health. Even today, products like hormone creams, that are, amongst other things, supposed to lessen wrinkles and restore a lost youthful skin, are suspected of causing cancer and other problems.

- Aluminium is often found in lipsticks. We used to think that aluminium was not toxic, although we now know to the contrary. Unfortunately lipstick is swallowed when eating, as well as being absorbed through the skin.
- There are other chemicals found in lipsticks, some of which can be mildly addictive.
- Dyes and other chemicals found in all coloured preparations can cause allergy problems.

If you have a really sensitive skin, but want to improve your looks and morale by using cosmetics, it is worth finding a brand that has as few additives as possible, that is as natural as possible and that doesn't cause you any itching or skin rashes. Alternatively, you could make your own; a quick guide to the cosmetic use of everyday natural substances is included at the end of this chapter in order to help you avoid many of the unnecessary chemicals. This guide advises on the long-term care and maintenance of the skin, nails, hair and teeth rather than short-term make-up. Short-term 'paints' can and should be removed when they are no longer serving their purpose, and definitely before going to bed at night.

Damage can occur through years of neglect and not looking after the skin, as well as by adding harmful chemicals. Not only have we found nothing that will magically restore young skin; there are also a number of things that make the skin, hair, nails and teeth look old before their time:

- Smoking is a great wrinkle-maker and can be guaranteed to age your skin as well as yellow your nails and teeth.
- Regularly eating too much sugar can be relied upon to rot the teeth.
- Skin and hair can also take on that weathered look if continually exposed to the elements without any care or protection.
- Exposure to too warm and drying central heating also speeds up the shrivelled prune look, so take care and economise on heat to save your purse and your skin.
- A poorly balanced or inadequate diet, along with insufficient exercise, will show itself in the condition of the hair, eyes and skin. For example, an insufficient intake of the essential fatty acids will definitely reduce the skin's glow, the nails' strength and the hair's lustre.
- Any chemical designed to give a dramatic effect should be used with caution; dyes, bleaches, rinses, perm solutions, depilatories and tanning preparations are some of the most obvious.

There is no known short cut to healthy skin; it needs looking after. All the essential secrets are found in natural substances, the secrets of which the cosmetic industry often try to copy. Allantoin, for example, is an effective moisturising agent found in face creams, but it is found naturally in the leaves and roots of the comfrey plant. Allantoin was once hailed as a miracle beauty treatment, and scientists now synthesise it from uric acid taken from cow's urine, which somehow makes it lose its enigma and appeal!

SCENTED WATER

Perfumed baths have been indulged in for centuries. Nowadays scented bubble baths are popular, but these are often made from synthetic chemicals and a considerable amount of soap which, between them, destroy the acid and bacterial balance of the skin. Herbal bath scents are in fact more desirable from the long-term health point of view. A scented bath can stimulate both you and the skin's pores; alternatively it can relax the muscles, soothe the joints and induce sleep. A little vitamin C powder or lemon juice will help to maintain the skin's natural acidity.

- Scents which are stimulating are basil, bay, fennel, lavender, lemon verbena, lovage, meadowsweet, mint, pine, rosemary, sage and thyme.
- Lavender has antiseptic properties and lovage is considered to be a deodorant.
- Relaxing herbs include catnep, chamomile, jasmine, lime flowers and vervain.
- Comfrey, lady's mantle, marigold, mint and yarrow have healing properties.
- Tired, sunlight-deprived winter skins are revived using nettle, daisy, dandelion or blackberry leaves.
- If your water is hard, a little sodium bicarbonate will help to soften it. Soft water, though not so healthy to drink, is better to bathe in.

MASSAGE

Massage is very important for any skin, even if you have to do it yourself.

A good rub with any edible cold-pressed oil softens and

protects the skin. Soy oil is often chosen because it has little smell, but corn, sunflower, safflower or wheatgerm oils, if they have not had their vitamin E removed, will do just as well, although they do not rub in as easily and have a slightly stronger smell. Let the oil soak in for a while, then relax in a warm, scented bath. The skin will shine. The skin will also be softer if a little honey is rubbed in as well, or if oatmeal is added to the bath.

DEODORANTS

We sweat as a result of fear, excitement or heat. The sweat itself has little smell, but subsequent bacterial action can cause BO. Deodorants are therefore often used, containing an antiseptic to kill bacteria and a perfume to disguise any that get away. Antiperspirants usually contain aluminium or, preferably, zinc salts, intended to clog up the pores and to prevent sweat from escaping. Some of these chemicals can cause irritation, especially if used after removing hair. It is also thought that excessive use may cause problems in the underarm glands. Excessive use of these products is therefore not desirable.

MOUTHWASHES AND TOOTHPASTES

Antiseptic mouthwashes or perfumed rinses are only temporary disguisers of bad breath (halitosis). Not only is this condition probably destroying your social life; it is also likely to be telling you something important.

It could be telling you that you do not clean your teeth properly and that there are still pieces of stale food left in between; that you have one or several bad teeth and need to see a dentist; that you have a medical condition that needs investigating by a doctor; that you are zinc or beta-carotene deficient; or it could be that you have eaten strongly flavoured food recently, like garlic, onions, cheese or spices. Foods, drinks and smoking also make your mouth taste as well as smell, so consider your intake, on romantic occasions in particular.

Toothpaste

Toothpaste is a relatively new multimillion-pound industry. On its good side toothpaste makes the mouth taste cleaner and fresher, and makes us brush our teeth more. On the bad side, however, toothpastes contain a lot of chemicals, some of which damage the teeth, others our health.

Toothpastes usually contain colouring and flavouring agents, binders, humectants, detergents, foaming agents and polishing chemicals (some of which may be too abrasive for some teeth). They may also contain anti-septics which can adversley affect our beneficial mouth bugs. Some contain desensitising chemicals to help sensitive teeth, or enzymes to control tartar.

Most toothpastes contain fluoride, and in such quantities that if a small child ate a family-sized tube the dosage of fluoride that he would get could be fatal. Make sure that you rinse all of the toothpaste out of your mouth, or use one of the herbal or home-made varieties.

JEWELLERY

Metal from jewellery may well be absorbed through the skin. Gold and silver are usually fine, but nickel can cause itching or rashes on sensitive skins.

Copper will also be absorbed. This is sometimes useful for arthritics if they are low in copper, and their symptoms may improve. However, if you already have an excess of copper, this type of jewellery is not to be advised as it could cause a related zinc deficiency.

COSMETIC USES OF NATURAL SUBSTANCES

- Almond. Moisturiser. Oil used to soften and moisturise skin and to eliminate dry or scaly patches. Ground almond used as a scrub to prevent blackheads, spots and enlarged pores.
- Angelica. Odour eliminator. Leaves used in baths, especially foot-baths. Root, when chewed, freshens breath, removes odour.

- Apple. Germicidal. Scent and antibacterial action make it an active ingredient of many hair, skin and hand preparations.
- Apricot. Very beneficial for the skin due to its high beta-carotene and polyunsaturated oil content. Used in anti-wrinkle preparations, and to prevent stretch marks and signs of aging necks.
- Avocado. Very rich in oil which penetrates the skin well; has healing as well as moisturising properties. Can be used on hair as well as the skin.
- Banana. Can be used as a skin cleanser, as can avocado.
- Bay. Antiseptic properties. Leaves used in baths and for making perfume.
- Beer. Excellent hair rinse, giving good shine.
- Bicarbonate of soda. Good cleanser; can be used in toothpastes.
- Blackberry. Astringent properties in fruit. Leaves soothe burns.
- Bran. As you might expect, bran is used as an abrasive scrub. It can also be used to remove grease and dirt from hair or skin.
- Camomile. Highlights white or blonde hair. Also a relaxant in a bath.
- Carrot. Juice has long been reputed to benefit skin, hair and eyes when taken internally. Has a mild, light tanning effect when applied topically.
- Castor oil. Nail strengthener.
- Cinnamon. Breath freshener. Can also be incorporated into home-made toothpaste.
- Cloves. Antiseptic and very characteristic smell. Good in baths or as mouth and breath freshener.
- Cocoa butter. Useful as a lip gloss.
- Coconut. Oil is used as a moisturiser; especially good for sore lips as it's edible. Can use it for cleansing, (commercially used in soaps) and as a suntan oil. It is a saturated oil.
- Comfrey. Healing properties. Good for chapped skin and as a bath soak.

- Corn. The starch is used as a dry shampoo. The oil, if it is cold pressed (not had the vitamin E taken out and an artificial antioxidant added) is good rubbed into the skin to soften it. Best rubbed in before a bath; then soak in the warm water, allowing the oil to penetrate; towel dry. Leaves the skin supple and shiny.
- Cream. Good for smooth skin, especially for moisturising around the eyes, which is a particularly sensitive area.
- Cucumber. Astringent, but very mild; suitable for sensitive skins. Valuable as a skin cooler after sunbathing, to soothe sore eyes, and as a skin cleanser, helping to prevent blackheads and spots.
- Dandelion. Good cleanser; sometimes used in baths, for cleansing properties rather than scent.
- Eggs. Egg whites 'stretch' the skin, so are good for keeping skin as wrinkle-free as possible for its age. Yolks are moisturisers and can be rubbed into face and hands. Egg as a shampoo gives hair body and shine.
- Elderflower. General skin-texture improver.
- Fennel. Soothes swollen and sore eyes.
- Garlic. Antiseptic. Also stimulates hair growth.
- Grapefruit. Good in skin treatments, softening elbows, knees etc. Because it's acidic, like lemon, it is good in the bath water or for a hair rinse. The skin and hair should be slightly acidic, and citrus juices are useful for restoring this mild acidity after washing, especially if soap has been used.
- Honey. A very effective softener with healing properties, good for spotty skins or rough, weather-damaged skins when applied topically. It is anti-bacterial.
- Horseradish. Good for skin blemishes. Extracts from the root will help to lighten age spots or freckles in some cases. It whitens nails. It does tend to dry the skin if used too often.
- Lavender. Often added to any preparation to provide a scent. Cleansing action.
- Lemon. Astringent. Like grapefruit, it restores the skin

or hair's natural acid balance. It is a good all-round addition, also providing vitamin C.

- Lettuce. Cleanser and natural mild tranquilliser.
- Lime. Flowers lighten the skin; have a calming effect in the bath.
- Marigold. Skin tonic. Also highlights red-brown hair.
- Melon. Cleanser; moisturiser.
- Milk. Long used to soften skin – queens used to bathe in it.
- Myrrh. Used as a treatment for mouth ulcers. Also in toothpastes, mouth rinses and skin toners. It was used to preserve mummies, so has preservative properties.
- Nettles. For tired feet and strengthening the hair.
- Oats. Used as a scrub for cleansing; also to whiten hands.
- Olive. Absorbs the sun's UV rays, so useful as a sunscreen oil. Good for brittle nails or hair.
- Orange. Another citrus fruit with an appealing smell (cf. lemon and grapefruit).
- Orris. Root is good for keeping teeth white, and as a dry shampoo.
- Parsley. Valuable as an anti-dandruff agent, hair rinse for dark hair and to control acne.
- Peach. Moisturiser for tired skins.
- Peppermint. Used in cosmetics for taste and smell; general use.
- Pine. Fragrance is often desired; good in baths.
- Potato. Reduces swelling and inflammation, especially of skin and eyes after sunbathing.
- Rhubarb. Reddish temporary hair dye.
- Rose. Used a lot for scent, but also good for chapped skin.
- Rosemary. Especially good for shining hair and to prevent dandruff. Also can be used in baths, etc., for its scent.
- Safflower oil. Even higher in polyunsaturates than sunflower oil; good for body massage (cf corn).
- Sage. Used to whiten teeth and strengthen gums. Stimulant when used on the scalp. Because of scent and taste,

can be used in mouthwashes, toothpaste, etc.
- Salt. Antibacterial; helps to heal broken skin. Although it can cause severe stinging when initially added, salt water is useful for very minor cuts and grazes.
- Sesame oil. Also tends to absorb harmful rays from the sun whilst allowing the tanning process, therefore useful as a sunscreen.
- Strawberry. Good for alleviating sunburn and whitening teeth. Also good for the skin.
- Sunflower. Oil is good for body massage (cf other oils).
- Tea. The tannin in tea, whilst not desirable in great quantities internally, is very good at absorbing the sun's more damaging radiation; it is therefore a useful sunscreen (though it washes off with bathing). Slightly dyes the skin, so helping you to look tanned. It is sometimes used to brighten dull dark hair and to relieve eye strain.
- Thyme. Bath additive and a shampoo.
- Tomato. Supposed to reduce the effects of large pores.
- Vinegar. Good as a hair rinse to make hair shine (diluted, of course, or it will also make it smell).
- Yoghurt. Like milk, it is good for skin preparations; also as a hair conditioner. It has antifungal properties.

Cosmetics should make us smell good, feel good, look good and do no harm.

21
HAZARDS IN THE GARDEN

Only 1½ per cent of the land in the UK is used for gardens. Despite this, gardening is one of the most satisfying and popular hobbies, occupying millions of people. It often provides much needed physical exercise, as well as relief from mental stress and tension. It provides us with an opportunity to be creative as well as to grow our own flowers and food.

A survey by the Ministry of Agriculture, Fisheries and Food found that around 90 per cent of all fresh fruit, cereal and vegetables for sale had been sprayed with pesticides. But in our own gardens we have the opportunity, if we wish, to grow fruit and vegetables that are free from these chemicals. We may not be able to grow all of our own food, but we can certainly supplement the food we buy with produce that is not only less contaminated but also has a higher nutrient content because it can be picked and eaten right away without it losing nutrients during storage and transport. This helps to reduce our toxic load a little.

SAFETY

Your garden should be a safe, happy and healthy place, but you will have to make sure it is.

- Be aware of uneven paths; loose slabs, stones, roof tiles or slates; revolving washing lines that turn in the wind and always seem to be positioned at eye level; open windows that are similarly positioned.
- Think about where you leave garden tools, rubbish (especially glass), hoses, tubs and furniture. Will they cause an accident?

- Are your paths slippery in wet weather due to algae, moss or lichens?
- Are your ponds and pools safe for children and pets? A child can drown in just 3 inches of water.
- Are such things as shears, secateurs, mowers and chemicals stored and used out of the reach of children and pets?
- Is all children's equipment – swings, climbing frames, etc. – on a grass, cork, wood-chipping or sand surface rather than on concrete?
- Are gates and fences secure, preventing young children and pets from straying on to roads and causing accidents?
- Manure and pet droppings can cause disease if improperly handled, so make sure that they are not accessible to small children.
- Sandpits are often used as a toilet by animals, so should be covered when not in use.
- Yoghurt pots or similar should be put over any sharp objects like canes.

ELECTRICAL EQUIPMENT

Electrical labour-saving equipment solves many problems in the garden, but causes others. Always remember that equipment for use outdoors should have weather-proof electrical connectors – it should be designed specifically for outdoor use.

Should you accidentally cut through a power cable – and you shouldn't if you are using the equipment properly – don't be tempted to pick up the two cable ends without switching off at the mains first. This may seem obvious, but it is surprising how many people don't think and do just that. Circuit-breaker sockets are a good idea as they cut off the current immediately if such an accident does occur, so preventing what could be a bad or even fatal accident. You really need an RCD (residual current device) for this, not one of the miniature pieces of equipment.

Most electrical equipment is also noisy and so causes noise pollution. Spare a thought for the neighbours, who may be trying to enjoy an outdoor lunch or to relax in peace and quiet in their garden while you are mowing the lawn on a Sunday afternoon. It is sometimes a good idea to have a time when you all mow the lawn, or whatever, at the same time, so that you do not cause each other irritation.

BONFIRE

Bonfires can, similarly, upset those living near you; having hung out all your washing on a lovely summer morning, there is nothing worse than finding your neighbour covering it with smoke from their bonfire. In some areas it is an offence to burn rubbish anyway; it is at least common courtesy to burn garden rubbish in the evening and to check wind direction and your neighbours' washing line or barbecue first.

Fires can cause severe irritation to some people, especially those suffering from chest conditions like asthma or bronchitis. Even log fires can sometimes cause problems for these people.

It is also essential that you do not pollute the air with toxic fumes from burning upholstery, foam or chemicals. It should go without saying that smoke from any fire should never blow over a road, where it could cause an accident, or into anyone's house.

BARBECUES

Barbecues are very pleasant on occasion, but foods cooked on them are not very healthy – the more charred they are the more carcinogens they are likely to contain. So don't overdo the cooking; perhaps part-cook conventionally first.

Breathing in the smoke from a barbecue is also not particularly desirable. Always use fuel intended for barbecue cooking, not paraffin, meths or petrol.

CHEMICALS IN THE GARDEN

It is obviously preferable to use compost rather than artificial fertilisers, and to avoid chemical sprays wherever possible, but it can be difficult to control pests and diseases without using anything at all.

There are really only two basic types of product that are relatively natural and have been used for years. One contains copper, and helps to control mildews, blights and rusts; the other contains sulphur, and helps to control powdery mildews and storage rots, as well as greenfly, blackfly, caterpillars and some beetles and mites. Both of these chemicals are used by the body and, although an excess can cause problems (as can an excess of anything), at least the body knows how to handle them. Soap has also been used for some time to control white, green and black-flies, and so, paradoxically, has concentrated cabbage water.

PLANTS THAT DEAL WITH PESTS

Plants themselves can be used to deal with garden pests.
- Parsley, for example, repels rose beetle, if you don't mind parsley in your rose bed.
- Garlic and chives repel blackspot, mildew and aphids.
- Hyssop repels blackfly, so can make all the difference planted next to your beans.
- The skins of cucumber repel woodlice and cockroaches (I only wish I'd known that when I lived in the tropics and frequently chased cockroaches away from my precious and hard to get potatoes.)
- Angelica stems scattered amongst your herbaceous plants deter earwigs.
- Wild Hellebore deters rodents.
- Mole plant, *Euphorbia lathyrus*, deters moles.
- Onions grown amongst your cabbages and lettuces deter rabbits.
- Ordinary ground pepper is very useful in deterring stray cats from using your freshly dug vegetable plot or green-house as a loo.

- Pyrethrum, *Chrysanthemum cinerariifolium*, can be used as an insecticide, controlling some mites, aphids and leaf hoppers.
- Nicotine (from *Nicotiana tabacum*) also tackles these pests, and whitefly as well.
- Quassia, from *Picraena excelsa*, controls mealy bugs, leaf hoppers, thrips and slugs. It is one of the active constituents of the Biofriendly insect spray.
- The other constituent of this spray, and also an active constituent of the Biofriendly pest and disease duster, along with sulphur, is derris, obtained from *Derris elliptica* and *D. malaccensis*. Derris controls aphids, leaf-eating caterpillars and mosquito larvae.

PLANTS FOR COMPOST

Some plants, like clover, lucerne and wrack (i.e. bladderwrack or *Fucus vesiculosus*, the seaweed), make very good compost, while others, like valerian, nettle, dandelion, chamomile, yarrow and the bark of oak, decompose more quickly than others and can be used as compost accelerators, rather than the chemicals that are available for this purpose.

PLANTS TO BE CAREFUL WITH

Some plants need to be treated with caution. Those that sting or have prickles or thorns are obvious, and you will probably already know these well. However there are others, less well known, which may cause rashes or skin irritations in some people. Many bulbs and the sap of poinsettia and euphorbia can cause allergy-related problems. The leaves of other plants like bamboo, borage, carrot, celery, chrysanthemum, cucumber, geranium, marrow, parsnip, radish, strawberry and tomato may give a skin reaction – itching or a rash.

Some plants are poisonous, though not usually fatally so unless an awful lot are eaten. These include the berries of laurel, cotoneaster, holly, ivy, juniper, mistletoe, nightshade, privet, spindle, sweet pea, wild cherry and yew; and the leaves of foxglove, nightshade, privet, rhubarb and spindle.

POLLUTION AT
WORK AND SCHOOL

22
THE SICK OFFICE

Accidents and ill health associated with workplace activities are becoming increasingly common, in spite of better health and safety laws. It is impossible to avoid every problem; indeed, many accidents or health problems occur simply because people are not doing what they have been recommended to do. For example, advice to wear ear protectors whilst using noisy machinery is often ignored because the resulting hearing loss may not be noticed until years, maybe even decades, later.

Each year there are around 30,000 accidents at work, over 600 of which are fatal. Much more common are the so-called minor sickness symptoms – head and back aches; nausea; dizziness; lack of concentration; visual disturbances; muscular problems; eye, nose, throat and skin irritations; minor infections; lethargy – all of which bring about increased absenteeism and decreased efficiency and productivity as well as a serious decline in morale and enthusiasm.

Some hazards will be obvious, such as working with heavy machinery or with particularly hazardous chemicals, but others are much more subtle, less obvious and very effective at making you feel out of sorts. We are still learning about these molehills that have a nasty habit of developing into mountains, but it is possible to pinpoint and to avoid, or at least reduce, some of these hazards. Quite apart from the central heating, humidity, lighting, materials and cleaning chemicals used in the office, and identified in the previous chapters on the home environment, there are the possible additional problems of air conditioning, and office gadgets like VDUs and photocopying machines. It is possible to overcome or minimise some of these problems that cause stress, muscular strains, visual problems, headaches, etc., with a minimum of effort and a resulting increase in efficiency and well being.

AIR CONDITIONING

It is important to get air conditioning right – that is, if it has to be installed at all. Just as it is no good having central heating turned up so high that it is uncomfortable, it is necessary that air conditioning makes air better, not worse.

Air conditioning should, ideally, maintain the relative humidity somewhere between 40 and 60 per cent. They are a source of contamination themselves as they contain refrigerant gases, so they should be cleaned and checked regularly; badly used and poorly maintained systems can cause more dust and bacterial problems than there would otherwise have been. Legionnaire's disease, though rare, is a classic example of an infection spread by air conditioning systems, but office colds can be spread very easily, as can any undesirable fumes from office equipment, inks and paper, etc.

Any air treatment, be it air-conditioning, air filters, fans, or simply open windows, should be altered depending on the number of people in the office and the degree of contamination. If the office is being painted or having a lot of visitors, more exchange of air will obviously be needed. Photocopiers and other electrical equipment that have brush motors could produce ozone and should, ideally, be ventilated to the outside, especially if the building is tightly sealed to conserve heat, and an air-conditioning system is in operation.

VISUAL DISPLAY UNITS

The older VDU screens are constructed in exactly the same way as a television screen, with a cathode ray tube (CRT). The picture is created by the left to right and up and down sweep of an electron beam. The beam strikes a layer of phosphors on the screen, which fluoresces.

There are electromagnets around the CRT which bend and focus the electron beam. These electromagnets create electromagnetic fields around the unit whenever the computer is switched on. The radiation becomes weaker with increased distance, but it is the magnetic component, which, it is feared, may be dangerous to pregnant women. Research is not conclusive, for it is obviously a difficult area in which to obtain evidence – one can hardly ask pregnant women to sit in front of screens for varying lengths of time during their pregnancy to see which ones have miscarriages or birth abnormalities. There are other possible reasons why VDU operators could be more prone to miscarriages.

- Bad posture can contribute to miscarriage in the early stages of pregnancy – sitting scrunched up in front of a screen (or, come to that, a typewriter or a desk) for long periods could be a problem for someone who is at risk.
- Stress, too, can alter hormonal activity and raise blood pressure, causing complications in pregnancy and even miscarriage.
- Ionising radiation is known to cause birth defects and miscarriage, the dose needed to do this varying from person to person; there is no known safe level of exposure to ionising radiation, it all has some effect. The VDU with a cathode ray tube produces ionising radiation, while the liquid crystal display units found in most portables do not.

There are other hazards for VDU operators:

Non-ionising radiation may well affect the male as well as female reproductive system, although research is still inconclusive. It was suggested at first that operators should wear lead aprons, but these do not provide protection from non-ionising radiation. It is also possible that overexposure to this type of radiation may cause cataracts. It is therefore best to limit your exposure to the unit, take breaks from it and don't sit in front of it whilst you are not actually working on it (i.e. if you are thinking, or talking to a colleague). Pregnant women, and more importantly those trying to become pregnant, should be able to transfer to alternative work for that period of time.

Electrical fields are also a problem, but are easier to deal with. For example, 8,000–20,000 volts are needed to form an image on a VDU screen, and screens with several colours may need up to 30,000 volts. This creates an electrostatic field which is positively charged. Human beings are also electrically charged, but the field we create is negatively charged.

To compound the problem, there is often a lot of dust and debris in the air, particularly in air-conditioned offices, and especially on a Monday morning when the air-conditioner has been switched off all weekend. All this dust, bugs and grime is attracted by the electrical field, and as most such particles will be positively charged it will be attracted to the operator's face. Some research has shown that dust deposits can be as high as 10,000 per square millimetre of skin per hour. This accumulation of dirt can cause skin rashes; sore, red, itchy and watery eyes; dry skin; and allergies. Some experiments with make-up show that this can be attracted away from the wearer's face and on to the screen, or, alternatively, it can be forced further into the facial tissues. There are now screens available which eliminate electrostatic charge, and reduce glare and reflected light into the bargain. These screens do not, however, alter the effects of radiation.

Skin rashes and red patches or blotches on the skin are common among VDU users. Those who already suffer from acne or dermatitis may find that their condition gets worse. Eye irritation is also common (eye problems and muscular problems are dealt with in the general section on page 121–22 as they are not exclusive to VDU operators).

PCBs (polychlorinated bi-phenyls) have been banned since 1986 as they are considered to be carcinogenic, but they may still be present as insulating fluid in older VDUs. Although they are not be a problem with newer machines, significantly high levels of these are found in the air of workplaces that use the older models.

When working with VDUs it is therefore worth putting a few simple preventative measures into operation.

- Only 4 hours in the working day should be spent at a VDU.
- Short 5-minute breaks every half hour are better than longer less-frequent breaks.
- Walk or move around during the breaks; use other muscles and give the tense ones a rest.
- Use an anti-static filter if possible; if not, at least use an anti-static wipe on the screen. The filter should help to remove glare and reflection as well.
- Make sure that furniture is suitable for VDU use and your comfort.
- Make sure that the screen is adjustable and doesn't flicker.
- Use a liquid crystal display unit if possible if you are, or are trying to become, pregnant. Alternatively use a screen that will scatter radiation to the side and not let it come directly at you (although there is no point scattering radiation to the side if there are other people working in that space).
- Use lots of plants to clean the air and restore negative ion balance. Cacti have been found to be particularly good at restoring this balance. A two-year trial was carried out in offices in Wall Street; one 40-centimetre-high *Cereus peruvanius* chandelier cactus was put next to each computer screen, and employees stopped suffering from continual headaches and tiredness and improved both physically and mentally.
- Remember that VDUs give off a lot of heat, so turn the heating down accordingly, or the atmosphere will become too dry.

VDUs are very useful, but they should be used responsibly to minimise their possible effects on health.

STRESS AND STRAIN

Stress

One person's stress is another person's strength. All sorts

of things may contribute to stress: no childcare provision; home worries; not getting on with one or a number of the rest of the staff; boring and monotonous work without sufficient breaks; work that you don't like; work that you feel that you can't cope with; too much or too little responsibility; too much noise; office chemicals; smoke; too little room. The list is endless. Only you know what causes stress in you. It is therefore a good idea to have a short break, once a month or so, where people can get together and say what is affecting them. Communication and cooperation goes a long way towards making a happier workplace.

Stress can cause many different symptoms, depending on the individual. When we become upset or irritated or feel trapped in an inescapable situation, our body chemistry changes to deal with that situation. We become very tense as the body prepares its muscles for action, only to be disappointed as the only action they get is to lift a coffee cup. Blood pressure is increased and sugars are released into the blood. Digestive juices and hormones change, and the nervous system gets geared up, making us irritable and jumpy, ready for the action that never comes. All this change and build up of energy causes symptoms, which may accumulate over the years to cause bigger problems.

To start with we may only notice that we tire easily, become irritable or depressed, have difficulty sleeping, perhaps lose our sex drive or develop PMT or other menstrual problems. We may get indigestion, regardless of what foods are eaten; we may feel sick or get headaches, or other aches and pains. Over a period of time the depression can increase; we become more accident prone; high blood pressure and indigestion become the norm; skin, digestive, heart and circulatory problems develop.

Some people bottle up their stresses and problems; others use a distraction technique, and busy themselves with other things. Not all stresses are avoidable, but having a positive attitude and trying to change those stresses that can be changed is a good start. If everyone works together on the changes that can be made – the office set up (lighting, furniture, etc.), the social environment, the employer–employee relationships, and the best utilisation of individual skills – the stress factors would be much less.

Muscular problems
Stress or psychological tension leads to muscular tension. Tense muscles are less efficient than relaxed ones, and more liable to be injured.

- Office workers are likely to suffer from backache and aching neck or shoulder muscles.
- Those using any form of keyboard are also likely to have pain in the fingers, hands and wrists.
- Workers who can't move around much are more liable to get pains in the feet, ankles and calves.
- Poorly fitting chairs that impair circulation for long periods at the backs of the thighs will also cause problems.

Immobility, or very restricted movement, is likely to cause as many problems as continuous, repetitive, pressurised movements. The aim has to be a reasonable balance of movement throughout the day.

Repetitive strain injury
VDU and other keyboard operators often suffer from what is termed RSI, or repetitive strain injury, caused by overuse of certain muscles and tendons, and resulting in inflammation in that area. There are different RSIs depending on the muscles or tendons involved.

- Tendinitis is inflammation of the tendons.
- Peritendinitis is inflammation of the area around the tendons.
- Tenosynovitis is inflammation of the tendon sheath.
- Bursitis is inflammation that affects the fluid sac (bursa) which allows ease of bone and tendon movement.
- Epicondylitis is this type of injury in the region of the elbow.

- Writer's cramp is when you actually experience cramp in the hand or arm.
- Carpel tunnel syndrome is when inflammation causes fluid and tissue in the wrist to press on nerves in the area.

RSI starts as a mere ache in the overused area, which is usually ignored and may go away, although it will come back with increasing frequency. Later the ache becomes a pain which continues even after work, and may develop into pins and needles or numbness and even cramps.

Prevention is better than needing surgery or suffering permanent disability, and RSI is completely preventable; 5-minute breaks every half an hour are better than one break mid-morning or afternoon. During any such break you should move around, not sit in front of the same switched-on VDU screen with a cup of coffee.

Eyestrain

Around 30 per cent of the population have eyesight that is defective in some way but has not been detected because they have not had an eye test. Problems sometimes become more obvious when someone starts using a VDU, typewriter or some other office equipment for a long period of time. It is also possible that a person's glasses, especially bifocals, or contact lenses are not suitable for VDU work – it's worth checking with the optician.

Common office eye symptoms are: blurred vision; seeing double; burning or sore eyes; contact lens irritation; aching or pain; intolerance to light; tiredness; headaches; even migraines or nausea. These may be caused by glare or reflection of VDU screens; if this is the case the problem can be minimised by using a filter screen made from a special nylon material which reduces reflections by 90 per cent. Adjustable screens are also better, as the contrast between the images and background can be altered, depending on conditions and on the operator. Screens that flicker are to be avoided, as they cause stress as well as eye irritation.

Lighting and daylight sources are important for all

office work. Position your desk in the best light for whatever you are doing. Fluorescent lights are best avoided, if possible, both from the point of view of the shadowless harsh light that they give and because of their side effects like noise and tendency to cause depression.

Eyestrain can be avoided by taking breaks during the day from staring at your work. This need not take a lot of time; you just need to find an object, either out of the window or at the other end of the room, that you can focus your eyes on occasionally. This simple exercise makes the muscles of the eye change the shape of the lens, the frequent change from long to short vision helping to keep the eye muscles and lens supple. As years go by you are then more likely to retain good long and short distance vision. Aching eyes can be caused by these eye muscles having to stay in the same position for long periods of time.

Noise
Noise is a very important factor which affects concentration and health. Any continuously noisy or really loud equipment therefore needs to be shielded in some way.

Smells
Smells are also a problem. Some people are very sensitive to photocopying smells and other inks and office chemicals, as well as to cleaning chemicals. Even simple things like solvent-based felt tips can be very potent and bring tears to the eyes, so remember to put lids on all of these potential smells whenever possible. Cigarette smoke, too, is likely to irritate; offices should be smokeless zones.

Remember that spider plants and cacti, in particular, but other plants as well, help to reduce the atmospheric concentrations of positive ions and less desirable gases like the carbon oxides; they therefore have a definite and valuable role to play in the workplace. They can be given as a present or to show concern and a desire to improve the workplace, as well as being morale boosters.

Temperature

Temperature and humidity should be varied according to needs, not fixed at standard settings. Humidity, in particular, is very important to people who wear contact lenses; air which is too dry may make wearing contact lenses intolerable.

OFFICE FURNITURE

Chairs

Any office needs well-designed furniture. A chair, for example, is useless if it gives you backache, lacks support in the vital areas, puts you in an unnatural position (many with high backs do this and cause neck problems) or gets in the way, e.g. some arm rests. Adjustable chairs are preferable if you are setting up an office, as they can be altered depending on the height of the person and the desk or equipment that they have to reach.

Desks

Desks should be positioned for the best light rather than for the look of the office, this usually being at right angles to the window (neither VDU screens nor their operators should face a window). Desks should have a matt finish if they are to be the home for a VDU, as matt finishes give less glare.

Desks need to be big enough to accommodate equipment and to allow room for papers and other work. It is also useful if it, or preferably a nearby windowsill, has room for a plant or two, especially the cacti which are very good at removing positive ions from the air, as mentioned earlier. But one word of warning; if you do have plants on a desk with a computer, don't overwater – the plant may not mind, but computers rarely take kindly to sitting in a puddle.

Carpets and cables

Carpets need to be anti-static if there are any computers in the room. Leads and cables need to be positioned where they cannot be tripped over.

23
THE SICK SCHOOL

Any illness or disease tends to affect the most vulnerable members of our society first – the sick, the elderly, pregnant women and children – and environmental illness is no exception. In children, symptoms tend to be hyperactivity, and learning and behavioural problems. Then, as they grow up, the symptoms change to lethargy, lack of concentration, lack of interest and, sometimes, destructive and aggressive behaviour. Allergies and their various symptoms are also common.

CHEMICALS AT SCHOOL

Most children go through a phase of being allergic to school, but this is usually mental rather than physical. In reality, most children have fewer allergy problems at school than at home, but some are sensitive to particular lessons.

- Art classes use materials like clay, paints, varnishes, paste, glues, crayons, various papers, inks, plants, aerosols, etc., all of which may affect a chemically sensitive child.
- Woodwork and metalwork will use paints, thinners, cements, varnishes, lacquers and plastics, and produce sawdust and wood shavings.
- Chemistry classes have the odours and fumes associated with using chemicals.
- Biology also has its share of potential allergens as there will almost certainly be plants and animals in the classroom.
- Even the ordinary classroom has chalk dust or solvent-

based pens for writing on the board.

Most children should be able to deal with this relatively small amount of contamination, but there are a few who have already reached the point of overload and do get symptoms. The best one can do is to reduce exposure to problem materials out of school so as to reduce the total load; to boost detoxifying nutrients to help combat the problem; and to try to pinpoint the allergens at school, even though they may not be able to avoid them completely.

PETS AND OTHER ANIMALS

Animals at home as well as at school – even someone else's pet – may cause allergic symptoms. Problem animals are usually the pets that have feathers, hair or fur. Snakes, fish, turtles and tortoises are often all right, but they aren't very cuddly; the real need for a pet is often to have a living thing of one's own to look after, hug, stroke and love.

Sometimes it is the saliva or dander (flakes of dead skin that all mammals shed) of the animal that starts the symptoms, and the cat and horse appear to cause more reactions than any other animal.

SCHOOL MEALS

School meals can be a problem for the allergic child. Maybe he sees his friends eating something that he fancies; either he may know that it will affect him, but he can't resist trying it all the same, or he may not realise that the food contains an ingredient that will affect him. Either way, he may suffer symptoms.

School meals can also be a hazard for the non-allergic child, who may be tempted to spend all his dinner money on crisps and chocolate bars rather than on wholesome nutritious food. Unfortunately, now the school meals service has become a commercial enterprise, financial considerations often come before the health of the young people. Crisps and chocolate bars make a good deal of profit: vegetables and salads – indeed any nutritious dish which takes time and labour to prepare – make little profit. Consequently, many caterers would turn down a school-meals contract if they could not sell the high-profit, processed, packaged, instant foods. The usual argument given is that it's what the pupils want, and the pupils should be able to choose the foods that they eat. This seems ridiculous, however. It's a bit like inviting pupils to come to school and then to give them the choice as to what they do; if they prefer to sit and do nothing, or to kick another child under the table, or to behave in such a disruptive way that no one else can get on with any work, then that's OK, that's their choice.

We know that children, and even teenagers, do not always make the best choices (it's often difficult for adults); that is why children, by law, are guided by adults until they are 18. It seems that school is a good place to learn what to eat and how to eat. There is plenty of time after school hours for pupils to choose to eat unhealthy nutrient-deficient food. These days many parents are both working, and have little time to prepare packed lunches; however they often believe that their child is getting a good lunch at school, little realising that their money is being wasted on empty, high-calorie nutrient-deficient rubbish snacks. Parents who are really concerned about the health and well-being of their children should get together and have the unhealthy snack foods removed from the school canteens.

ENVIRONMENTAL PROBLEMS

There are a range of other problems under this heading.
- Perhaps the school is situated close to electricity pylons, or a tip, or a dirty factory.
- Maybe there are problems associated with the buildings themselves – plus the use of air conditioning, central heating, artificial light, television, VDU screens, etc.
- Noise is another, often missed, pollutant which is

particularly applicable to children. Continual noise should be discouraged, as it can cause over-stimulation as well as learning and behavioural problems.

POLLUTION WE CONSUME

24
FOOD
PRODUCTION

In the western world we have the advantage of access to plenty of nutritious food. Unfortunately, however, we either remove a lot of the essential nutrients by processing or we treat it with toxic chemicals. What we tend to forget is that whatever we put into other creatures and plants stands a good chance of eventually ending up in us. Even if we do not eat the living things that have been contaminated, other creatures may eat them; in this way the contaminants pass up the food chain so that we eventually end up consuming them. The first animal in the food chain may eat only a small amount of a pesticide, for example, but a larger animal may eat several of the smaller animals and so accumulate more of the chemical; or perhaps a cow will consume a lot of grass that has been sprayed with fertilisers to make it grow well, and thus ends up storing a lot of fertiliser residues. Man is at the top of the food chain and so gets a greater dose of the poisons accumulated because of this biological amplification.

The general public trusts that what they are being given is nutritious food; we assume that the people employed to look after our food know what they are doing, and put food quality and public health before other concerns. However there is some doubt over the use of many chemicals and processes used in the production of food. Obviously, no one sets out deliberately to poison or deplete the food; but now that we understand some of the problems, it is important that the professionals in the food field ensure that the public are given nutritious food and not deficient or poisoned rubbish. The good health of the people and the planet must come before the material gain of the minority.

It is not only the problem of the professionals in the food industry; other industries produce rubbish which contaminates our fresh and sea waters, as well as the land and air, so that, in turn, our plants, fish and other animals are contaminated.

THE PROBLEMS

Nitrates

With intensive farming comes the application of fertilisers. Unfortunately there is a tendency to overdo these, which means that some are not used by the plants and seep into our water. As a result, nitrates are becoming a problem; and may be found in milk, for example, if the pasture on which the cows have grazed has been treated with nitrate fertilisers. They are also a problem when they seep into our ground water.

Vegetables normally obtain the nitrates they need from the soil and convert them into protein. When plants are forced with a lot of nitrate fertiliser, however, much more nitrate than is necessary passes up the stems and is stored, ready to be converted into protein, with the result that vegetables are often picked to eat in this state, i.e. very high in nitrates. The crops most likely to suffer from this are those grown out of season, especially those that are grown in a greenhouse with reduced light (there is always less natural light in winter), as nitrates are not readily converted under these conditions. Stems tend to be particularly high in nitrates, leaves less so, and the roots not very much at all; our natural seasonal root crops are therefore a better buy than forced lettuce and tomatoes during the winter.

Beer, wine, processed meats and reheated foods all tend to contain high levels of nitrites; processed meats, in particular, are treated with nitrites to improve their flavour, to add colour and to act as a preservative. An acid medium helps to prevent conversion of nitrites into harmful nitrosamines in the gut, so when eating or drinking these products it is wise to include natural acids in the diet, such as vinegar, citrus fruits, tomatoes, rhubarb, etc. Vitamins C and E also inhibit this conversion.

In fact it is not so much the nitrates themselves that are a problem, but the nitrites and nitrosamines that they are turned into in the body that cause the damage to body tissue. This conversion happens in all of us to some extent; smokers, however, have about four times as much thiocyanate as non-smokers, and thiocyanate is a catalyst which helps to convert nitrites to nitrosamines. Smokers, therefore, are much more prone to nitrosamine damage.

Pesticides

There are no food labels for added pesticides. Unfortunately, although we may all prefer to eat residue-reduced foods, we can neither see nor taste the pesticide residues, and so it is difficult to know whether we are eating them or not. In fact, the average person gets through about a gallon of pesticide a year in or on his food and drink, and walking or living in the country or near a carefully kept municipal park may increase the exposure if pesticide spraying is frequent.

Indeed, the problem is now so bad that pesticides are found in mother's milk. Once ingested, pesticides are stored in our and other animals' fat layers, so that fat in milk and meat will be higher in pesticides than the aqueous or lean portions. In grains the highest residue levels are found in the bran. In fruit and vegetables it is on the skins; some of these may be removed by washing with a weak vinegar solution, or, of course, by peeling.

To be sure, pesticides have contributed to our improved health by reducing the incidence of food poisoning, for example, but there is a very fine balance to be achieved in this area. One of the worst problems is that of mixed pesticides, where we may ingest several different pesticide residues, and the resulting mixture of these chemicals causes an entirely different set of reactions to those produced by each of the chemicals taken separately.

Dosage is the all important factor. Oil for industrial use is often heavily contaminated with pesticide, the assumption being that it will not be used for eating. Seeds which are destined for planting are similarly treated, and cannot be eaten. But accidents have happened, where people have consumed such oils or seeds, resulting in deaths from acute poisoning. Many more people are victims of chronic poisoning from pesticide residues whereby small, but almost daily, doses of toxic substances accumulate in their body and eventually produce long-term symptoms.

There are several different types of pesticide:

- Pyrethroids are natural pesticides derived from the chrysanthemum family, although they can now be produced synthetically. They are easily broken down and so are probably the safest to use; they are not very toxic to man and are soon removed from the environment. However, they are toxic to bees and fish.
- Carbamates are also used as pesticides. The main problem with these is that they are readily changed to harmful nitrosamines in the stomach.
- Organochlorines are very persistent in the environment, remaining as a contaminant for years after they have been used. DDT, lindane and the aldrins belong to this group.
- Organophosphates are less persistent in the environment, i.e. they are broken down more easily. However, they will cause acute poisoning if taken in excess, as they are basically nerve poisons. Organophosphates inactivate choline, a vital neurotransmitter, so that memory and concentration are impaired. They also prevent uptake of manganese (heavy liming of soil is also antagonistic to manganese). As manganese is vital for the production of enzymes needed for detoxification, manganese deficiency exacerbates the problems of pollution. Deficiency of manganese in children often leads to what is commonly known as growing pains (pains in the limbs for no apparent reason).

Are the pesticides really worth their potential cost? It is the consumer who pays the highest price, not in money but in health.

Hormones

There has been extensive use of hormones in livestock rearing, although this is now declining. Stilbenes (synthetic female sex hormones) were once used a lot in meat rearing; they were used in chickens, in particular, to produce capons – male birds treated with female hormones to make them a more convenient size for family meals. Such use is now banned in theory, as it was found that it caused cancer and birth problems. The hormones were also found to accelerate the aging of bones, in children in particular.

Hormones that are still used, however, include the following:

- Thyroxin increases milk yield in cows, and wool yield in sheep.
- Progesterone may be given to sheep, pigs and cattle so that they give birth when it is convenient to us.

Other growth promoters

- Anabolic steroids have been used to make meat leaner.
- BST (bovine somatotrophin) is under scrutiny at present; it is a protein which increases milk production per cow, so that a farmer can own and feed less cows but still maintain the same milk production.
- Copper can be added to the feed of pigs to increase their weight before they are sent to slaughter; it is only added at this time because, otherwise, the excess copper would be stored in the liver and cause the animal's death.
- Arsenic is also used in animal feed as a growth promoter.
- Antibiotics are used to make young animals in particular, and especially chicken and calves, gain weight. Antibiotics are also still used to kill harmful bacteria, of course, but because of this routine, rather than necessary, use, there are now many bacteria that are resistant to antibiotics. This is very worrying as bacterial diseases will become harder to control effectively.
- The feeding of livestock with cheap animal-protein feed pellets is not only unnatural but has also led to a lot of

infection, livestock deaths and human disease. Public concern is currently focused on mad cow disease (bovine spongiform encephalitis, or BSE), which may well have arisen as a result of this sort of practice.

Food is vital to our health. Convenience and cost should never come before our needs. We must be very careful when proposing anything that alters the natural balance in food production.

THE FOOD

Fresh foods are best and generally less contaminated than the processed stuff. However, all food becomes less nutritious with storage, especially when exposed to light, heat and air. Most perishables are best stored in a fridge, sometimes even in an airtight container; lettuce, for example, will keep much longer in an airtight container in the fridge than it will uncovered in the fridge or in a cupboard. Bottles of cold pressed oils are far better refrigerated, and so is wheatgerm.

Fish

Nuclear waste, concentrated sewage, toxic chemicals and industrial waste all find their way into fish, especially the freshwater fish that live in our misused rivers. Even deepwater seafish are not free from the ravages of dirty man, although they are less polluted than the shore-loving varieties.

Chicken

The life of the chicken is one of the most interfered with of all our agricultural livestock. If it is fed antibiotics to prevent infection and increase growth rate it may be hatched, grown and eaten in eight weeks. A free range chicken, in contrast, has to be housed and fed for longer as it grows at the normal rate and hence lives for longer before it is the right size for eating.

Chickens often live on a litter of wood chips. As a result, wood preservatives, especially pentachlorophenol, can be found in the livers of these animals. Furthermore, food colourants like tartrazine may be added to chicken-feed to make the egg yolks yellower. Free range eggs are not subjected to this sort of treatment, and are higher in the essential fatty acids than are factory-farmed eggs.

Meat
Animals may be dipped in pesticides, which often cause temporary symptoms in the animal. As we have seen, the fat of any animal acts as a store for pesticide residues. When we eat such contaminated meat our body fat does the same. The more fat we eat and store, the greater our potential for storing pesticides.

Milk
The fatty, creamy portion of whole milk will be higher in pesticides than skimmed milk. Milk will also sometimes contain antibiotics given to cows to prevent mastitis; such milk should normally be discarded, but it isn't always. Milk products like yoghurt and cheese will not have this problem, however, as the antibiotics would ruin the bacteria that make the cheese or yoghurt.

Fruit and vegetables
These, fortunately, are no longer allowed to be coloured, but they may still contain pesticide residues. If you go to a pick-your-own establishment, always ask where you should be picking; fruit may look better in one area rather than another, but it could have just been sprayed. There is a time limit between spraying and harvesting or eating, and you could become ill if you ignore this time lapse.

Washing fruit in weak vinegar solution removes some contaminants. Peeling will also remove some surface contamination, so if you eat a lot of fruit, it might be wise to peel some of it to balance your roughage and pesticide intake. Alternatively, you could buy organic food, even if it's only some of the time.

25
FOOD ADDITIVES

The first additives used were those that made it look as though you had more than you actually did; for example, the addition of water to milk, beer or wine, and rusks and other fillers to meat products to make them go further. This was dishonest and misleading, unless it was declared and the price reduced accordingly, but at least it was not harmful. Some additives, however, did cause health problems; 18th-century tricks included the addition of brick dust to cocoa, sand to sugar and alum to flour.

Nowadays food manufacturers are much more subtle, but even so, we still have what sometimes amounts to legalised poisoning. Many of our food additives are not foods at all; they are chemicals used to make us think that we have more of the product that we think we are buying; or to make things look fresher than they actually are (e.g. pink colouring added to stale or rusk-diluted meats); or to mislead us into thinking that we have something that we do not (e.g. pink colour and strawberry flavour added to a so-called strawberry product that has never contained any real strawberry). Additives can be used to make food taste better, look better, feel better and to provide extra nutrients (as in the case of added vitamins).

One of the more subtle problems with food additives is that they can be used to make the same basic ingredients into almost any meal you like – by altering the colour, the flavour and the texture. This, of course, means that, although you always appear to be having a varied diet, you may in fact be eating the same old monotonous and low-nutrient starch mixture all the time – very unhealthy and unbalanced.

There are around 4,000 different food additives that can be used, and we use over 200,000 tons of them a year.

Many have not been tested for safety, so we are only gradually coming to realise the side effects that they are causing. The effects of combinations of these chemicals is also unknown, yet we may consume as many as 20 different chemical additives at one sitting. Only a few hundred have to be named on a label if they are used as ingredients; most do not have to be declared at all, or only need to be group-listed – for example as 'flavouring' – without any indication as to which chemical is used and how much of it.

Even the words 'natural additives' are not necessarily safe. Natural poisons abound; arsenic and cyanide are natural, but we wouldn't wish to take them as supplements. Other natural additives are not natural to our usual diet. For example, are the eggs and ovaries of the cactus beetle part of your normal diet? They are used to produce cochineal, E120. The seed pod of the bixa tree is also unlikely to feature regularly in the everyday diet, yet this gives us the natural additive anatto. Have you ever tasted flamingo feathers? These give foods a natural, orangey-pink colour.

Labels, far from revealing the facts, can be notoriously difficult to interpret. Strawberry-*flavour* dessert has no strawberries: strawberry-*flavoured* dessert must contain some fruit. Orange *juice* contains fruit: orange *drink* contains less fruit: orange-*flavour* drink contains no fruit. It makes shopping and eating very complicated.

COLOURS

These are used to make things look attractive, fresher or the right colour for the added flavour. Citrus fruits used to be coloured to make them look better, but this is now illegal; no fresh fruit, vegetables, meat or fish can now contain any added colour. However, processed fruit, vegetables, meat or fish, and their products, may all contain colours.

Some colours are natural, and even desirable in reasonable amounts; for example, beta-carotene is a precursor of vitamin A, riboflavin is a B vitamin, and chlorophyll is a naturally occurring green pigment. Many others are harmless in normal quantities, like lycopene and betanine, which are natural extracts of tomatoes and beetroot respectively.

Other colours, though, are less desirable and even positively harmful. They can cause hyperactivity in children, bedwetting and antisocial behaviour, whilst some like aluminium, E173, are cumulative poisons. All synthetic coal tar and azo dyes are best avoided, especially by children and people who have problems with allergies.

Permitted colours are labelled from E100–E180. Some colours have been withdrawn and others limited in their use due to the adverse effects that they are thought to have. The colours withdrawn from consumables intended for children are, in numerical order:

- E104, quinoline yellow.
- E107, yellow 2G.
- E110, sunset yellow.
- E122, carmoisine.
- E123, amaranth.
- E124, ponceau 4R.
- E127, erythrosine.
- E128, red 2G.
- E131, patent blue V.
- E132, indigo carmine.
- E133, brilliant blue.
- E151, black PN.
- E154, brown FK.
- E155, chocolate brown.
- E180, pigment rubine.

E173, aluminium, and other chemicals which may contain it, like E541, E554, E556, E558 and E559, are also best avoided, as it is known that aluminium accumulates in the brain, thyroid, liver and, sometimes, bones where it can cause a whole range of symptoms over the years, memory loss and dementia being the most serious.

E150 or caramel is really chemically treated burnt sugar; but whilst the caramel you make at home may be fine, the mass-produced stuff is now suspected of causing immune damage by reducing white blood cell production and robbing the body of vitamin B6.

FLAVOURS

Many consumables now boast the 'free from artificial colours' label, but how about the flavours? Most processed food is of poor quality; that is the very reason why it is processed and not sold as the prime stuff. This means that it needs something to make it appealing. Natural colours may be able to disguise the look of the product, but how about that inferior taste? Flavours and flavour enhancers or modifiers are therefore used abundantly.

- 'Strawberry flavour', for example, means no strawberry.
- 'Nature identical flavour' means chemical.
- 'Natural flavouring' means added natural flavour, and may include nature identical.
- 'No artificial flavour' may mean that a natural flavour has been added – perhaps bits of cactus beetle.

There are some 3,500 flavours in use, and they do not have to be declared; indeed, they may not even have been tested for safety, although some work is now being done on them. For years, though, we have been eating foods that contain additives that may well have been damaging our health. We assume that, because food manufacturers are in the business of providing food, they know what they are doing, and only put foodstuffs into our food. It seems that we have been wrong, however, and that they add anything that makes their product cheaper and more appealing. Only food should be permitted in our food; such things as aluminium and flamingo feathers have no business being in foodstuff at all.

Sometimes chemicals are added to take away an unwanted taste or smell. Margarines, for example, need to taste roughly the same every time they are made; yet often a different mixture of oils and additives is used in different batches, so the taste and odour have to be removed and then the generally accepted taste and smell added afterwards. Biscuits are the same; they need to taste and feel the same so that, whenever we buy a packet, we know exactly what they will taste like.

Flavour enhancers are also used to bring out the natural flavours. Salt and sugar are two obvious examples of these, but some, like monosodium glutamate, have a more sinister reputation. The chemical enhancers commonly used are:

- E620, L-glutamic acid.
- E621, monosodium glutamate.
- E622, monopotassium glutamate.
- E627, sodium guanylate.
- E631, sodium 5-ribonucleotides.
- E636, maltol.
- E637, ethyl maltol.

Flavour enhancers are used extensively in take-away foods, Chinese and Indian in particular, so don't have these too often. Monosodium glutamate is banned from use in baby foods, because it was found to cause brain damage in rats; however, many highly flavoured packet snacks that seem to be freely eaten by toddlers do contain this and other additives undesirable for young children. It is better to use the old tried and tested flavour enhancers like orange and lemon juice (citric acid), vinegar (acetic acid) and yeast extract (as long as you are not sensitive to yeasts). The glutamates, in particular, may cause dizziness and palpitations as well as causing gene damage if used excessively.

PRESERVATIVES

Preservatives are used to make sure not only that the food itself does not go off too quickly but also that the additives do not go off; for example, preservative is necessary to make sure that the red dyes stay red and the blue colours stay blue. Other preservatives are used to ensure that a particular flavour will last and will not deteriorate rapidly; this is especially important if the food is to have a long shelf-life. Even products that you would not think needed preservatives, perhaps because they do not contain ingredients like meat that are at risk of going off, could be heavily laced with additives if they contain artificial flavours and colours. If a product has a very long shelf-life and yet boasts no preservatives, it has probably had all the potential nutrients taken out so that not even bacteria or moulds would want to eat it, in which case it's not worth buying. Remember, we have to consume food in order to give our bodies the necessary nutrients. Food without nutrients isn't worth buying, and a high-calorie low-nutrient diet can be a positive danger to health.

Numbers E200–E290 denote preservatives.

- Benzoates are common preservatives, but should be avoided by anyone who suffers from asthma, skin conditions or hyperactivity (E210–219).
- Sulphites (E220–E227), too, can be dangerous to asthmatics or allergy sufferers, as they destroy vitamin B1. They may be hidden in wine.
- Nitrates and nitrites are very common, especially in cured meats. They can form nitrosamines in the body, especially if the vitamin C intake is low. Nitrosamines have been linked to cancer, possibly due to the fact that they reduce the body's available oxygen. It is therefore wise to limit your intake of nitrates and nitrites.
- E300–E321 are antioxidants; they help to slow down the normal oxidation process that occurs when food is exposed to oxygen in the air. In other words, they help the food to keep longer without deterioration. The gallates, BHA and BHT, are artificial antioxidants which have been associated with many health problems, including cancer.

Antioxidants and preservatives which prevent the growth of bacteria and moulds are sometimes very important and necessary, and definitely preferable to the presence of bacterial and fungal poisons. But artificial preservatives that prevent deterioration of colours and flavours should be dispensed with, along with the chemicals they are supposed to preserve.

Fruit contains a lot of vitamin C, which is a natural

antioxidant, while oils contain vitamin E, also a natural antioxidant. Unfortunately, many oils have had the vitamin E removed and an artificial antioxidant added instead; this happens particularly with the commercially prepared oils because they keep longer with the artificial antioxidant than they do with the natural one. This is all very well in the bottle, but our bodies prefer the natural antioxidant; they know what to do with it, whereas they cannot necessarily cope with the synthetic antioxidants. It is better to use cold-pressed oils, as the cold-pressing process ensures the vitamin is not damaged or removed.

E300–2, E304 and E306–9 are all types of vitamins C and E, and as such are to be preferred to any other preservatives and antioxidants.

EMULSIFIERS AND STABILISERS

When fat needs to be mixed with water to give a nice even constituency, an emulsifier has to be used, and very often a stabiliser, too, to make sure it stays evenly mixed and does not separate out again. Egg is a natural emulsifier, because it contains lecithin. In processed foods, lecithin (E322) alone may be used, derived from soya bean; this is a perfectly good emulsifier, as are the lactates, tartrates, citrates and the alginates (E325–E337).

Some emulsifiers are laxatives and can cause intestinal damage. They are often linked to gut problems and food allergies and, in the extreme, are thought to cause liver damage. It seems sensible, therefore, to limit intake of foods containing these less desirable emulsifiers, mainly those in the E430–E450 range, and E385. Carageenan is also suspect; it has been withdrawn from use in its degraded form, but there is concern that it may be converted into the degraded form during some methods of processing.

Emulsifiers are necessary to ensure a good texture for some food; we all use emulsifiers, even in our home cooking, for example when we make egg custard or bake cakes. Commercially, however, emulsifiers have been abused, especially now that they are being used to make high-fat meat look like the leaner stuff; emulsifiers hide the fat nicely and, if anything, improve the texture, so be wary of eating too many of these processed meats.

SWEETENERS

The obvious sweetener is sugar, seen most often as white sucrose. However, these days there is also a market for the darker raw sugar, which is less refined sucrose and has the advantage of containing small amounts of other nutrients such as B vitamins and some minerals.

There is nothing wrong with sugar, as such; the body knows how to deal with it – it is its main fuel. Sucrose, once absorbed by the body, is broken down to glucose, and it is in this form that it is utilised by the brain and other tissues and organs. The problem is that we eat too much sugar, often in the refined form, without the other nutrients needed for its proper utilisation, and often without doing enough exercise to use it up. Too much sugar causes a strain on the metabolism, and ultimately gets stored as fat.

The problem is exacerbated by the fact that sugar is often hidden in the ingredients of processed foods. It is useful stuff – because it's quite cheap, it adds weight, it acts as a preservative and it improves texture; it is therefore used in savoury as well as sweet dishes. It may be labelled as corn syrup, dextrose, fructose (fruit sugar), glucose, glucose syrup, golden syrup, hydrogenated glucose syrup, honey, invert sugar, lactose, mannitol, molasses, sorbitol, sucrose or xylitol, although sorbitol, mannitol and xylitol are more correctly termed sugar alcohols.

Artificial sweeteners are often cheaper than sugar and have less calories, so they are favoured by manufacturers. However they may cost a lot more in terms of health. Cyclamates were once used, but are now banned in many countries as they are considered to be a danger to health if consumed regularly for long periods. Saccharine, too, is now suspected of being carcinogenic if consumed regularly over a long period. Acesulfame gives an increased cancer risk and raised cholesterol levels in animal studies. Isomalt and thaumatin are also used to provide sweetness, but what else might they do to us?

Aspartame is made from a combination of two naturally occurring amino acids, aspartic acid and phenylalanine. There were therefore high hopes for its use as a sweetener, but even this is now suspect. It is a problem for sufferers of phenylketonuria, for example, and studies on air pilots have linked it with memory loss, confusion, visual problems, headaches and gastrointestinal problems. Consuming too much aspartame can upset our amino acid pool upon which protein metabolism is dependent, and taken in excess it is broken down into methanol and thence to formaldehyde, a very potent preservative which could pickle you from the inside. On top of all this, cancer cells (in particular, those that are present in skin cancers) love phenylalanine.

It seems there is no safe and healthy substitute for sugar; the only alternative is good old-fashioned willpower.

SOLVENTS

Flavours and colours are often evenly distributed in a product by the use of a solvent. These solvents do not have to be named but they are present in significant quantities in a processed diet. In particular, they are present in high quantities, as much as 20 mg/kg, in solvent-extracted decaffeinated tea or coffee.

WATER, BULKING AGENTS AND PRICE

Polyphosphates are used to increase the water content of processed and frozen fish and meats; it is, after all, cheaper to sell water than it is to sell chicken or ham.

Furthermore, bulking agents can be added to processed foods in order to make it appear as though you have more for your money. By and large, processed food is much more expensive, weight for weight, than the same nutrients available from unprocessed food. If you think about it, this has to be the case; it takes time, machinery and additional ingredients to process food. It is an illusion that the processed meats and instant dinners are just as cheap or cheaper than real food, processed food is almost always made from the poorer quality ingredients.

Get into the habit of counting nutrients rather than judging by weight alone. For example, we did a calculation using crisps, taking a £3.50 sack of potatoes as our control; the same weight of crisps as the sack of potatoes would have cost us £150 i.e. £6,000 per ton. We also did a similar calculation on the price of an orange fizzy drink. At the time, the price of Thames water was 34p per cubic metre, while petrol, which we all complain is far too expensive, was £450 per cubic metre. In contrast, the fizzy orange drink would have cost £2,000 per cubic metre.

We all need more *real* food, without any unnecessary additives.

26
WHAT WE DRINK

Healthy drinking is very important. We are, after all, around 70 per cent water, and use up this precious chemical, daily, in very many ways. Long term, it has been shown that, as we age, we sometimes lose our sense of thirst; if this happens our brains can develop air pockets where there should be fluid, and this can cause memory loss, often corrected by regaining the desire to drink.

Why do we drink? Which are the best drinks? Which should be used in moderation? What do they contain? There are many drinks on the market, but some do not quench the thirst as well as others, and some of them contain undesirable additives.

WHY WE NEED TO DRINK

We drink to obtain vital liquid. In fact, water will always suffice, and is sometimes preferable, biochemically, to our commercially prepared drinks. However, for thousands of years now, people have consumed flavoured drinks. Some even have health benefits, as they provide extra nutritional minerals.

- Water is needed to carry the nutrients that we extract from food to the areas of the body where they are required.
- It is also needed to take away the waste products that are produced.
- Water is needed to make up the fluid in which all of our cells are bathed, and to facilitate diffusion of both food and waste across the cell membranes.
- Almost all our biochemical reactions require water, at least as a solvent, maintaining a vital ion balance.
- Water is also needed to make up the many body fluids

such as blood and lymph, which have to carry not only chemicals but also structures like blood cells, around the body.

- Our body's central heating system depends on fluid distribution, while sweat enables us to cool down when necessary. Our bodies are thus maintained at a temperature which supports life, thanks to water.

WHEN WE NEED MORE FLUID

Exercise generates heat, and we then lose water from the lungs as well as from the skin; the more exercise we do, the more water is needed to replace that which is lost. In cases of extreme exercise, minerals are needed as well because, when the body sweats, it loses minerals as well as water. If the body sweats profusely, so that the sweat is dripping off us, too many minerals may be lost.

Environmental temperature is also a controlling factor in our fluid requirements. In hot dry climates we sweat more than in cooler, more humid, conditions, and so need more to drink. This applies equally to indoor air-conditioned centrally-heated environments as it does to climates.

If we are ill we need more fluid, in order to dilute the toxins produced both by the bugs that are attacking us and by our own bodies as a result of the battle. If there is fever – a high temperature, resulting in copious perspiration – or diarrhoea, we need to replace the lost fluid. Fluids are also needed after any sudden shock, stress or change – an accident, operation, hangover, childbirth or giving blood – while chemical changes in the body often increase the need for fluid.

Some of our fluid requirement will be met in the body as a byproduct of metabolism, some will be taken in the form of food – plant material, in particular, contains a lot of water – but most of our liquid is taken in as drink.

DRINKING WATER

Water is an obvious first choice. We are fortunate in this country in that we have water that is safe to drink; it is very rare for our tap-water to contain bugs that will cause disease. However, few people drink it unflavoured.

Bottled water is becoming increasingly popular. Fizzy water, in particular, is a pleasant change, and usually contains less bugs than still water; however, once opened, such water should not be kept for too long as it becomes stale, just like food. Still bottled water is sometimes better than tap-water, sometimes worse, depending on the area in which you live. Check the labels on bottled water, as some are higher in salt or fluoride than others and these are not so desirable.

Check too, with your local water company to see what is in your water; whether they use aluminium sulphate as a flocculant, for instance, and what the chlorine residual and mineral content is. Healthy water should contain adequate levels of calcium and magnesium and low levels of antinutrients such as aluminium, lead and cadmium. It should certainly not have high levels of pesticides or nitrates.

A few people are very sensitive to the chlorine used by most water companies to get rid of bacteria in water. These people may need to avoid tap water and instead drink bottled or filtered water. But filters are not always reliable, as you never know when they have become ineffective. An alternative is to boil the water or allow it to stand in the open air; the chlorine will then disperse, although some of its chemical combinations will remain. Very chlorine-sensitive people may even need to neutralise the bathwater by adding a teaspoon of sodium thiosulphate before getting in.

TEAS

Over 80 per cent of the UK population drinks tea – it is our national beverage, and has been drunk in Britain for over 300 years.

Tea leaves come from an evergreen shrub, but it is only the bud and two top leaves of the plant that are used. These are dried and then rolled or crushed so that sap and enzymes are released which cause the leaves to turn brown. Whilst this 'fermentation' is going on the leaves are kept cool, but when the process is complete the leaves are warmed up again and dried completely, turning black in the process and giving tea leaves as we know them. It is then blended to get the flavour right, using leaves from other crops, but no additives, as such, are added. Tea bags, however, do add to the tea whatever is in the paper of the tea bag itself; some tea, for example, made with tea bags was found to have high aluminium levels. This may not apply to all tea-bag teas, but it is probably better to use loose tea most of the time.

Tea is a reasonable source of manganese, but also contains caffeine, theophylline and theobromine which are oxygenated purines commonly found in plants. These are stimulants and, if used in excess, can be addictive; however if used in reasonable amounts, as found in weak tea, they can calm or stimulate effectively.

Herb teas
There are many herb teas, derived from various plants and reputed to have various beneficial effects.

- Alfalfa tea is supposed to be good for those with over-acidity, as it is alkaline.
- The oil contained in aniseed tea aids pancreatic enzymes and so, indirectly, digestion.
- Chamomile is a natural relaxant. The tea contains reasonable amounts of calcium, magnesium and potassium.
- Comfrey tea made from the young green leaves contains allantoin – very beneficial where healing is necessary, to the extent that it even reduces scar tissue. As a tea it particularly benefits those with ulcers, coeliac disease or other gut damage. It is also said to reduce adhesion formation.
- Dandelion tea is a good source of beta-carotene, choline,

potassium, calcium and iron. It supports all of the eliminating organs, including the skin.

- Equisetum tea is very strong and should not be used often. It is the richest natural source of silicon oxide; this is especially useful for improving hair, skin and nails. It has been reputed to soften or dissolve body gravel or stones, and to dissolve thickened tissue like adhesions or fibroids.
- Fenugreek tea is considered unpleasant by most people. It is very bitter, but is helpful when you have an infection. The flavour can be improved by adding lemon, but it is not a tea to drink regularly, and does cause perspiration.
- Flax tea soothes irritated bowels.
- Gingseng tea stimulates the pituitary gland and is not recommended for children, especially if they are already hyperactive; it is more for lethargic adults.
- Hawthorn tea can be taken regularly, and is especially good for the overstressed workaholic who has high blood pressure and insomnia.
- Hibiscus tea. There are about 200 different types of this tropical flower, and they all have different properties. However, all of them can be used as a 'cheer you up'.
- Hops are generally used for more potent drinks, but can be used as a tea. It has a calming effect, so is not to be taken by the lethargic. Even in its non-potent form it can be addictive, if taken on a regular basis.
- Jasmine tea is one of the most popular herb teas, both the green leaves and the fragrant white flowers being used. It is supposed to stimulate the desire to make love.
- Juniper tea is beneficial for the elderly who have a decreased hydrochloric acid output from the stomach, as it stimulates the production of this acid. It is not recommended for pregnant women or those with kidney or other gut problems.
- Lemon balm induces perspiration, so is probably more useful in hotter climates. It is advantageous for those who suffer from cramp.

- Lemon grass is a very popular and pleasant-tasting mild 'pick-me-up' tea.
- Linden or lime tea is sometimes used as an antidepressant, as it has a marked calming effect. However it should be taken with care, as it tends to slow the heart beat (beneficial for some but not for others).
- Liquorice tea acts as a mild laxative.
- Maté tea is not really advisable, as it contains strong stimulants like caffeine, as well as a lot of oxalic acid. It certainly should not be taken by anyone who has urinary gravel or stones, and should only be taken weak, if at all.
- Nettle tea is very beneficial for the lethargic, but should be avoided by the hyperactive.
- Parsley is nutritionally very rich. It has very high levels of vitamins A and C, as well as being a good source of calcium, iron and potassium. It is excellent as a food, as well as a tea.
- Peppermint tea is very refreshing and good for the digestion, as well as for respiratory problems, the menthol oil, still present in the dried leaves, being the therapeutic agent. The instant varieties of this tea do not contain the menthol oil, so are merely drunk for the flavour. As some of the flavour is also destroyed during the processing, artificial flavours are often added, making this instant tea a less desirable choice.
- Raspberry leaf tea is of particular benefit to pregnant women, especially near their time of labour, as it is a good source of copper and iron (copper levels are raised just before delivery, this change being necessary to bring on labour). It is reported to lessen morning sickness, as well as labour pains, and to help restore abdominal muscles after childbirth (provided exercises are also used, of course).
- Rosehip tea is made from the dried crushed seeds extracted from the rosehip fruit. Rosehips, as most people know, are very high in vitamin C, but this is tied up in a coating, and boiling water is necessary to release it. Rosehips are also high in iron and the bioflavenoids;

they can therefore act as a stimulant, so it's ideal for those lacking energy or trying to give up coffee, but not such a good idea at bedtime.

- Rosemary tea improves the circulation, and is said to improve brain function and memory, but it shouldn't be drunk too frequently and not by those who already have high blood pressure.
- Sage tea reduces perspiration and fever, and is generally calming. It is said to slow the flow of breastmilk, especially when drunk cold, so it should not be used whilst breastfeeding, but may be useful when the baby has been weaned.
- Thyme contains an antiseptic oil, thymol. This is released when heated, and can relax throat muscles. It is good when you have a respiratory infection, but is too strong to be drunk on a regular basis.
- Valerian tea is a valuable natural sedative and tranquilliser. It is, however, very strong in these respects and so should not be given to children unless they are very hyperactive.

There are many teas to choose from and probably the best advice is to find a selection that suit you and to vary them. The above is only a general guide as to their uses; if they are to be used because of any particular medical condition, more in-depth knowledge should be sought first. Remember, anything taken to excess is bad for you; balanced intake is the key to health.

COFFEE

Coffee trees produce small red fruits which contain the seed, or bean, as it is sometimes called (coffee beans are, of course, not true beans at all). The beans are roasted at around 250°C to give us the dark brown coffee beans as we know them.

Some beans are decaffeinated before roasting, usually by soaking them in a solvent. The obvious advantage is that these beans do not contain the stimulant, caffeine, but the disadvantage is that they will probably contain some solvent. If you are going to drink coffee, it is probably best to use it without solvent extraction and to get used to drinking it weaker or in moderation.

Instant coffee has already been percolated and filtered. It is then either:

- Spray dried – sprayed with hot air from the top of a tower, so that the solid coffee power falls and is collected at the bottom; or

- Freeze dried – solidified by lowering the temperature to −40°C, then warmed in a vacuum to get rid of the water.

The absorption of thiamine is adversely affected by caffeine, and it renders another B vitamin, inositol, ineffective, so addicted coffee drinkers need to ensure extra supplies of these vitamins, to be taken without the interference of coffee. Coffee robs the body of calcium, and so, over a lifetime, could induce bone problems unless rectified.

There are no additives, as such, in coffee, unless it's been decaffeinated; however we often add the additives ourselves, in the form of sugar, artificial sweeteners and milk or cream substitutes. For example, coffee whiteners are made of glucose syrup (i.e. sugar), vegetable oils (usually saturated palm or coconut) and milk solids; their fat content is thus almost completely saturated. Artificial sweeteners have their own associated hazards, as seen in the previous chapter; personally I think it is probably better to sweeten coffee with sugar, and gradually try to reduce the intake – taste buds do change with practice.

Chicory is used as a coffee extender or a coffee substitute. It is quite high in beta-carotene and choline, and is especially good for those with liver problems and high cholesterol.

FRUIT JUICE

Real fruit juice is squeezed from the fruit, but has a very short shelf-life – it needs refrigeration, and needs to be drunk soon after squeezing.

In order to make fruit juices keep longer, in particular

to enable us to drink tropical fruit juices that would not stand the journey to Britain, fruit is often crushed in its country of origin, filtered, evaporated, pasteurised and frozen for its journey. On reaching this country, the concentrated liquid is then mixed with water in order to bring it back, as near as possible, to its original concentration. It then has to be pasteurised again before it is packed, usually in aluminium foil-lined cartons, the foil lining being treated with a layer of polythene so that the acidic fruit juice does not come into contact with the aluminium. There are usually no other additives in the juice, though.

Fruit drinks, however, may contain a lot of additives, so juice is always the better choice. Squashes have even more additives; indeed, they may not contain any fruit juices at all. Whatever base is used for the squash is mixed with sugar or artificial sweetener and various colours, flavours and preservatives to make the final product. Many soft drinks contain sodium in the form of sodium citrate, which gives flavour and adds the fizz; soda water contains a lot of sodium, for example. These drinks should therefore only be consumed in moderation, if at all, and should of course be avoided by those with high blood pressure or heart problems.

Anything that is labelled 'drink' e.g. orange drink or fruit drink, may have only minute quantities of actual fruit juice, even if they say that they are made with real juice. A common alternative is '40 per cent juice', and this means what it says; 40-per-cent drinks are therefore much better value for money as there are at least some nutrients in them. The artificial stuff rarely provides anything much of value at all, just calories and artificial chemicals; they are, in my opinion, a complete waste of money, and probably do more harm than good.

Fizzy drinks, again, contain mainly water and sugar or artificial sweetener, along with other additives – colours, flavours, preservatives, carbon dioxide, emulsifiers and acidity regulators. Cola drinks are very popular, but it is not advisable to drink them in large quantities on a regular basis because of their high caffeine and sugar content. The kola tree is related to the cacao (cocoa) tree and produces fruit pods containing the cola nut. Extracted cola syrup is diluted with carbonated water and pasteurised, but, even diluted, it contains around seven teaspoons of sugar per can.

Fizzy and other soft drinks are all right in small, occasional quantities, but are not a good idea on a regular basis. And diet drinks contain so few nutrients that even bugs don't bother to grow in them!

COCOA

The seeds found inside the cocoa pods are allowed to 'ferment' for nine days after being picked. They are then dried, shipped to the consumer country, cleaned, crushed, roasted and ground. The cocoa fat or butter is extracted, and what is left is ground into cocoa powder, as we know it. There are no additives in cocoa powder, but drinking chocolate and other chocolate drinks may have several, and will certainly be high in salt and sugar.

MILK

Milk is a very good drink, not nearly as bad as the soft drinks, but it has, unfortunately, been given a bad name recently for two main reasons.

The first is because of BST or bovine somatotrophin. This is a genetically engineered hormone given by injection or implantation to some test cows, to boost milk production; the milk from these cows, it is alleged, is then mixed with normal milk. The fears are that the hormone could affect humans in some way, and that it could mask the fact that a cow is sick. Milk production usually goes down when a cow is ill, but if the production is kept up artificially then it could not only affect the health of the cow, but the illness could, perhaps, affect the milk and so affect us. It is wrong that anything should be added to our food or drink without our knowledge; we should not be used as guinea pigs without consultation or consent.

The use of hormones and other unnecessary medication on animals or plants that are to be used for food should be actively discouraged. BSE or mad cow disease, again caused by man, has also caused fears as to whether it could be passed on in the milk. This now seems unlikely, but if man had not fed cows on foods that were unnatural to them (animal protein) the problem would not have occurred in the first place.

The other main milk scare is the fact that it has quite a high fat content – particularly saturated fat – and its products, like butter and cream, have a very high fat content. Diets high in saturated fat are, in turn, linked with heart and circulatory diseases. Milk is, however, only 3.8 per cent fat, and we can now buy half fat and virtually no fat milk. (Milk is only around 3 per cent protein, contrary to popular belief that it is a very high protein food.) Milk is about 87 per cent water, and contains valuable vitamins and minerals; children would be better off drinking skimmed milk than colas and other soft drinks. Unfortunately government subsidies on whole milk mean that it is whole milk that is used in school canteens, as there is a better profit margin – another case of wealth before health. But it should be remembered that we do need fat in the diet. It is too much fat that is a problem; if we could rehabilitate our junkie cows and get away from overprocessing, milk would be very good.

Of our milk, 99 per cent is heat treated in some way, usually pasteurised by heating to nearly 63°C for 30 minutes or to 72°C for 15 seconds. This kills the bugs that are likely to do us harm. Sterilised milk is heated to 115°C for 20 minutes under pressure, while UHT milk is homogenised and then heated to 138°C; both of these keep longer, but their xanthine content will be higher, vitamin content lower and taste changed. Milk substitutes may say vegetable fat on the label, but often they contain more saturated fat than milk itself, and they usually also contain sugar (glucose syrup).

ALCOHOLIC DRINKS

Alcohol is a drug, but at least the body knows how to deal with it. Fermentation of some food by bacteria in the gut produces alcohol (ethanol), so even if we do not drink alcohol at all, we may absorb around 2 measures of it a day by this method.

Our liver produces an enzyme called alcohol dehydrogenase, which detoxifies alcohol. It is a zinc dependent enzyme, and usually we have enough zinc to make it. However, when we start drinking alcohol there may not be enough zinc to make the enzyme properly; the liver can only detoxify roughly one measure of alcohol every half an hour to an hour – above that it becomes much less efficient.

A few points to remember

- A unit of alcohol is half a pint of beer, lager or cider, a glass of wine, or a standard single measure of spirits. It is recommended that men consume no more than 21, and women no more than 14, units per week.
- There is no problem drinking small amounts of alcohol, but if taken to excess it first alters the body's chemistry and behaviour and eventually, if excess is consumed regularly, can permanently damage some tissues in the body, the brain and liver in particular.
- Alcohol is fattening – all the excess calories you take in are stored as body fat, so a weight increase is likely if you consume a lot of alcohol. A glass of dry wine has around 80 calories, a sweet one 100 calories, a measure of spirits 60 calories and a pint of lager, beer or cider around 160–200 calories.
- Although alcohol is a drink, it actually causes dehydration as less ADH (antidiuretic hormone) is produced, and this causes an increase in urine production. Part of the hangover symptoms can be attributed to dehydration.
- Alcohol is not the stimulant it appears to be initially, as its net effect is as a depressant.

The effect of alcohol on your body varies, depending on your sex, weight, what is in your stomach, what you drink and how quickly you drink it.

- The smaller you are the quicker you get drunk.
- Women absorb alcohol faster when they are either menstruating or ovulating, and have a higher blood alcohol level than a man of the same size.
- Fizzy drinks speed up alcohol absorption. Diluting alcohol with fizzy mixers has the opposite effect to what you might expect. Non-fizzy drinks do dilute the alcohol, help to prevent dehydration and thus lessen the symptoms of hangover.
- Sugar delays absorption of alcohol, but low calorie drinks do not.
- Food slows absorption of alcohol: you get drunk faster on an empty stomach. Carbohydrate and fatty foods, in particular, slow down its absorption.
- Alcoholic drinks of less than 13 per cent alcohol are absorbed slower than those above this level.

Ethanol itself is not the only problem. Most of us know our own alcohol limit, and sensibly control its intake. But there are other additives to alcoholic beverages, and these are not always labelled. For example, the darker the colour, the more likely the drink will contain other chemicals, sometimes called cogeners. These chemicals contribute their own symptoms to hangovers; hence the hangover is often worse with red wines than white. We could do with stricter labelling laws for drinks in this country.

Beer

Beers and lagers are very popular drinks; in Britain alone we drink around 30 million pints a day. It would, however, be very useful if the beer bottles and cans gave more information as to what's inside; for example, the aluminium, sodium and fluoride content of some beers may be high, depending on the water used. And what materials were used in production? Some beers are filtered through asbestos to clarify them – although this would not be necessary if we did not use nitrogen fertilisers, as it is these that make the beer so cloudy, as well as introducing the possible risk of nitrosamines.

Additives like preservatives, clarifying agents, pesticides and other chemicals – to control beer head and composition of the water, to reduce carbohydrate loss and protein degradation – are all often used. Gibberellins – natural hormones extracted from a fungus of the species *Gibberella* – may also be added to the barley to make it larger. Other additives include acetic acid, agar, benzoic acid, calcium chloride, calcium hydroxide, calcium sulphate, carageen, cellulose, citric acid, dimethylpolysiloxane, ethyl 4-hydroxybenzoate, furcellaran, hydrochloric acid, lactic acid, magnesium sulphate, methyl 4-hydroxybenzoate, orthophosphoric acid, phosphoric acid, potassium bromate, potassium bisulphate, potassium chloride, propane-1-2-diolalginate, propyl 4-hydroxybenzoate, silica, sodium alginate, sodium bromate, sodium hydroxide, sodium sulphate, sulphur dioxide, sulphuric acid and tannin. And you thought that you were drinking beer!

All of these additives are not bad, of course, and many just add to the mineral content, but there are people who could be sensitive to some of these ingredients. For those of us who like to know what we are drinking, the information should be available somewhere, even if only in the library, so that we can make an informed choice if we want to. It is a relief to know that there is a consumer group, the Campaign for Real Ale, which campaigns for beers brewed in the traditional way, using natural ingredients and producing real ale.

Wine

Before the days of refrigeration, preservatives and heat treatment, wine was a very good way of making a drink that would keep and was safe. Nowadays, however, all sorts of other ingredients are added, to the extent that some notorious imported wines had antifreeze (diethylene glycol) added to them, resulting in a number of deaths –

but how do consumers know what has been added to their wine? The information should be displayed on the bottle, surely?

Some of the additives used include ammonium sulphate, bentonite clay, blood powder (dried), calcium carbonate, carbon dioxide, casein, charcoal, citric acid, copper sulphate, diammoniumphosphate, egg white, gelatine, kaolin, malic acid, pectolytic enzymes, potassium bicarbonate, potassium disulphate, potassium ferrocyanide (fortunately only to red wines, so you can avoid this one by sticking to white wine), potassium kaolinite, potassium metabisulphate, potassium tartrate, silicon dioxide, sorbic acid sugar, sulphur dioxide and tannin.

Traditionally, wine is made by crushing the fruit (usually grapes). Yeast then ferments the natural sugars, producing alcohol and giving off carbon dioxide. Nowadays wine is very different, although there are some organic wines that boast traditional methods of production.

27
FOOD
SUPPLEMENTS

There are many factors that increase an individual's requirement for extra nutrients: genetic make up; state of health; infections; excessive exercise; medical drugs; industrial and agricultural poisons and emotional disturbances, to name a few. All of these call for an increase in vitamin and mineral, but not necessarily calorie, intake.

In our modern polluted world we have many enemies of good health. Our natural food contains many protective nutrients, but we often refine out a lot of these; and the more pollutants we are exposed to, the greater the dose of nutrients we need to provide protection. In Britain people tend to eat too much nutrient-deficient food, which in turn often leads to an excess of body fat and a deficiency of the micro-nutrients like the vitamins and minerals mentioned above.

We are also exposed to far more radiation and toxins than our bodies were designed for. Soil depletion has caused crops to be nutritionally inferior, and spraying with toxic chemicals increases our body load of pollutants. We tend to pick produce before it has fully matured and then use chemicals to ripen it artificially or delay ripening, as the case may be. The constant chemicalising of our food – with additives, bleaches, dyes, waxes, detergents, flavours, emulsifiers, binders – all increases the need for nutrients to detoxify the body. Even the excessive use of food substances like sugar can increase the need for vitamin and mineral intake, (cf. sugar p. 167).

VITAMIN AND OTHER NUTRIENT ANTAGONISTS

- The air pollutant, ozone, and smoke antagonise vitamin A.
- Nitrates, from high nitrogen fertilisers, will deplete vitamin A reserves, both in the food and in the body.
- Mineral oil binds Vitamin A and renders it useless to the body.
- Heat, excess sugar, excess alcohol intake, and antibiotics will deplete the body of thiamine, vitamin B1.
- Exposure to light or heat, excessive intake of alcohol, and the taking of antibiotics or hormones will antagonise vitamin B2.
- Excess sugar or alcohol consumption, heat, antibiotics and infection will deplete vitamin B3.
- Food processing and heat, as well as steroid hormones, destroy vitamin B6.
- We also need more vitamin B6 with age. Aging causes a decline in levels of this vitamin in the body, as do high protein diets – anyone eating a high protein diet needs more of the vitamins A and B6.
- Oral contraceptives and alcohol destroy folic acid, which will also be depleted by stress, surgery and vitamin C deficiency.
- Biotin is antagonised by avidin (in raw, but not cooked, egg whites), heat, alcohol and antibiotics.
- Sugar and alcohol antagonise choline, essential for good memory function.
- Antibiotics destroy inositol.
- Methyl bromide, a common insecticide found in food, totally destroys pantothenic acid.
- Many things destroy vitamin C – aspirin, steroids, stress, surgery, smoking, alcohol, sugar, heavy metal intake (like lead, cadmium, etc.) and car exhausts, to name but a few.
- Vitamin E is antagonised by oral contraceptives, food processing, stale fats and oils, mineral oil and inorganic iron.

Counteracting the antinutrients

Free radicals, heavy metals, nitrates, pesticides, radiation and smoke are all unavoidable pollutants. We can organise our lives to minimise them, but rarely can we avoid them completely. We can ensure some protection by increasing our intake of those nutrients that will counteract them or render them harmless.

Sufficient nutritional minerals like calcium, magnesium, zinc and selenium for example, will render aluminium, arsenic, cadmium, chlorine, fluorine, lead and mercury less toxic. Either they will be taken up by the body preferentially, instead of the toxic minerals, or they will stop them from doing any damage.

Antioxidants like the vitamins A, C and E are invaluable in rendering free radicals stable and hence harmless. Intake of these vitamins therefore needs to be increased considerably if you have to live or work in an area of high air pollution (including a smoky office). These vitamins also protect us, to some degree, from radiation. They are essential additives to foods like oils, as they delay the onset of rancidity; unfortunately the natural antioxidants are often removed from such oils, and an artificial one added which may increase the shelf life of the food but which is not so desirable for the body. The antioxidants, along with the minerals, zinc, selenium and manganese, are also important in the detoxification of pesticides by the liver.

Vitamin C is very good at preventing the formation of nitrosamines from the excess nitrates that may be in some of our foods.

Natural pectins, found in such foods as apples, bananas and carrots, are also very good at holding on to heavy metals and preventing them from being absorbed.

WHY FOOD SUPPLEMENTS?

Many of our foods contain the nutrients detailed above, but if we have a high exposure to pollutants they may not supply enough. Food supplements are becoming increasingly popular as people try them and notice how much better they feel. It is important to remember, however, that we are all different; we all need different amounts of these substances, and taking too much can be just as harmful as not having enough. It is the same with food itself. There is nothing wrong with sugar or salt, they are both essential; our problem is that we often eat too much of both. There is, fortunately, a lot of leeway and the body is good at adapting. Most of the time we will be short of one vitamin/mineral or the other, or else have one or two in excess, but this will constantly be changing, depending on our diet and our body intake of pollutants.

It is a good idea to look at your diet to make sure that you are getting all of the essential nutrients. Certainly if you eat a lot of the packet, tinned or processed foods, you probably aren't getting all you need, and require a supplement to replace the missing nutrients. If you live and/or work in a polluted environment you may also need supplements to counteract the effect of the pollutants. If you only have temporary exposure to heavy pollution, protective supplements may be useful for the duration of the exposure and for a while afterwards. Similarly, an infection or mental stress could deplete your reserves and provide a need for some sort of supplementation.

Vitamins

The vitamins required to counteract pollutants are primarily A, C and E.

Each day we need around 7,500 iu beta-carotene – a precursor of vitamin A, and the best form to take unless you are diabetic, in which case you cannot utilise beta-carotene and need the vitamin A itself. However, when needed, up to 20,000 iu can be taken.

Usually 1 gram a day of vitamin C is protective, but, again, when faced with excess chemical or microbial pollution, much more may be temporarily necessary. Diarrhoea is the harmless signal that you have taken enough of this vitamin.

Vitamin E supplements should always be increased

gradually, not suddenly, 100 iu being a good starting point and 400 iu being a reasonable intake if you feel you have a pollution problem.

Minerals

Some minerals are very valuable in combating pollution. They may act by being taken up instead of the pollutant, or by being part of an enzyme that is necessary for detoxification of that pollutant.

Calcium intake is vital; a supplement of around 300 mg per day is usual to provide protection. Daily consumption of 150 mg of magnesium, 5 mg of zinc and 2 mg of manganese is also advisable. Selenium is needed, as its intake is low in this country, due to low levels in the soil; however it is very toxic itself, even in relatively small doses, so whilst it is wise to ensure some intake, it isn't a good idea to err on the side of excess – 25 micrograms per day is plenty.

Amino acids

Two amino acids are sometimes recommended when there is evidence of accumulated toxins, these being L-cysteine and L-glutathione. However, they should be taken under the direction of a medical practitioner.

SMOKING

If you smoke you should be supplementing your diet at the higher end of the scale and should add some of the B vitamins, too, in particular vitamins B3 and B5.

SUGAR

If sugar is your vice, again the B vitamins should be taken as a supplement, to enable pollution levels of this otherwise useful food to be disposed of properly. Refined sugar, in particular, depletes the body of the B vitamins, especially vitamins B1, B2 and B3, as well as chromium.

If you eat a lot of sugar, it is therefore a good idea to cut down, while at the same time taking a vitamin B supplement in some form (tablets, yeast or wheatgerm).

SUPPLEMENTS AND THE IMMUNE SYSTEM

If you always seem to be a favourite host for cold and flu bugs, or for any other germs that are doing the rounds, your immune system could be out of tune. If you want to do something positive to improve the situation, rather than just suppress symptoms, you could try food supplements to get yourself back in control.

Viruses cause many of our commonest infections, colds and flu being the best known. Strictly speaking, though, viruses are not alive; they need to invade living cells in order to survive as they cannot reproduce without help. Once inside these cells they take over, and make the host's cells produce new viruses. If the viruses can be prevented from entering the cells in the first place, however, they will eventually be destroyed by cells of the immune system as they circulate around the body.

Vitamin C is a very good booster for the immune system; when most animals are ill they increase their manufacture of vitamin C. We humans have lost the ability to make our own vitamin C; instead we need to obtain extra supplies from our food. Unfortunately, most of the food we buy has been stored for some time, with the result that much of the vitamin C has been lost; and if we then cook the food, even more of the vitamin C content is destroyed. So when we are ill, or even when we want to prevent an infection, it is wise to supplement our intake of vitamin C.

If your cells have sufficient beta-carotene, the precursor of vitamin A, and found in particular in orange vegetables, then it is very difficult for invading viruses actually to get into the cells in order to replicate. As we have seen, they stay in between the cells, without doing any damage, until your white blood cells come along and get rid of them. Sufficient calcium and magnesium are also needed to keep your cells strong against attack.

Children and the elderly are more prone to viral attack. Children use up a lot of their vitamin A in growth and in the maturation of the immune system. On top of this they often eat fast foods which are low in nutrients and high in nitrate compounds (used for colour and preservation) which destroy vitamin A in the body. Children also use up lots of calcium in bone growth. The elderly often have a calcium/magnesium imbalance, and certainly need extra supplies of vitamin A to increase the activity of their diminishing thymus gland. For all these reasons, therefore, both groups need extra beta-carotene.

As the temperature falls at the onset of winter, all of us are less able to utilise vitamin A. So be prepared; before this high-risk time for viral invasion, take a course of vitamin A (about 15,000 iu), vitamin C (about 1 gram above your usual dose), calcium, magnesium and zinc. If you are in contact with someone who has a cold, or you feel the start of possible symptoms, then dive in right away with more of the same ammunition. Sucking zinc pastilles is the best way to take zinc if you already have a cold or throat infection.

If you catch an infection early enough, and counteract it with these simple, effective and useful supplements, you may prevent the infection altogether – but it requires very speedy action. If you succumb to an infection, these supplements are equally important, as the body needs these nutrients in order to maximise its defences.

ADVICE ON TAKING SUPPLEMENTS

In many ways supplements should be treated in the same way as medicines.
- They should be stored carefully in a cool, dark place.
- Dosage instructions should not be exceeded.
- Expiry information should be followed.
- They should not be used indiscriminately if you are taking prescription drugs.
- They should be free of all unnecessary additives.

Supplements may cause some symptoms, for example, diarrhoea with too much vitamin C, or an involuntary eye twitch with excess vitamin B6. The B vitamins and vitamin C may turn your urine a very bright yellow if you are taking quite a large dose.

Most supplements are best taken with meals. However single amino acids should be taken alone, or at least without any other protein. A mixed amino acid supplement is probably no better than eating a piece of meat or fish; it's merely more expensive and less tasty.

28
WHAT'S YOUR MEDICINE?

A medicine is a substance used to restore or preserve health. We often think of medicines as drugs, although in reality many of our everyday foods, drinks and habits expose us to drugs: tea, coffee and colas contain the drug caffeine; tobacco contains the addictive drug nicotine; and our wine, beer and spirits contain the even more addictive drug ethyl alcohol.

Sometimes medicinal drugs are necessary in order to control a disease or to restore the body's normal balance. As all disease either is, or causes, a disturbance of the normal structure, activity and/or function of some of the cells in the body, it is very useful and desirable to have drugs which can help to keep the body under control when necessary. It has to be questioned, however, whether it is wise to use drugs when they are not necessary. Some drugs are administered when they are neither wanted nor needed by the recipient, while others are taken voluntarily when they are not really needed. Furthermore, many medicines merely suppress symptoms and do nothing to effect a cure, while many more can cause problems of their own if misused.

Many medicines can be bought over the counter for self-medication. These are usually for what we consider to be minor problems which we do not wish to bother a doctor about. The main remedies are:

- Painkillers, taken for period pains, headaches, bad backs, etc.
- Cough, cold and congestion treatments.
- Pastilles, syrups, antiseptics, etc., for treating minor infections.

- Anti-diarrhoea and anti-sickness preparations.
- Laxatives.
- Slimming pills.

Are any of these medications any good? Are there any problems with self-medication?

GENERAL PROBLEMS

- Over-the-counter drugs, generally, merely suppress symptoms until the body has cured itself. Symptoms are the body's way of dealing with the problem, as we shall see later; to suppress them, therefore, is to put the body at a disadvantage, i.e. it makes the condition worse, or slower to rectify.
- You can be lulled into a false sense of security, thinking that everything is fine, when in fact the medication is masking a potentially dangerous condition. Antacids, for example, if taken daily, could mask the warning chest pains of an impending heart attack. Such medicines are all right taken on odd occasions, but no self-medication should be taken for more than 5–7 consecutive days.
- Medicines can react with each other, so it is not good to mix several remedies. Neither is it a good idea to add a home remedy for something minor if you are taking prescription drugs. Sometimes even apparently harmless things in them cause problems – diabetics, for example, may forget to consider the sugar content of a cough syrup.
- Many remedies cause drowsiness and many contain alcohol – so read the label before downing a whole bottle of cough medicine and then driving a car.
- Taking pills or medicines can cause psychological as well as physical dependence.

ANTIBIOTICS

Some drugs do cure. Antibiotics cure by killing invading bacteria (not viruses) that make us ill. They only destroy bacteria, so there is no point taking an antibiotic for a viral infection, although in the past they have been prescribed, just in case. Equally, there is no point taking antibiotics for a very minor bacterial infection that the body can deal with easily, for bacteria and the body get used to antibiotics; if they are taken too often they may become ineffective just when we may really need them.

If you have a course of antibiotics, all of the good, helpful bacteria in your body will be killed, as well as the baddies, and your B vitamins will be seriously depleted. It is therefore wise to consume yoghurt or lactobacilli supplements to replace the beneficial bacteria, and to take a course of vitamin B complex after you have finished the course of antibiotics, the dosage being 50–100 mg of the major Bs. (Biotin, folic acid and B12 are only consumed in microgram amounts, so don't be tempted to take any more – follow the instructions on the bottle.)

ANTIPYRETICS

These drugs bring down high temperature, examples being aspirin and paracetamol, and the children's mixtures containing these drugs.

When we have an infection our white blood cells have to work very hard to get rid of the offending bugs. As part of this defence process the body raises its temperature, simply because the white blood cells work faster and better at the higher temperature. Furthermore, bacteria are put at a disadvantage by the elevated temperature. These are thus two excellent reasons for having a fever when we are ill. Why interfere with the body's normal mechanisms for dealing with the problem, and delay the process of getting better by taking antipyretics?

COLDS AND FLU

Symptoms of a cold or flu – a stuffy, runny nose; raised temperature; headache; muscle aches and pains – may all be relieved by using a medicine to dry up the fluids, an antipyretic to control the temperature and painkillers to relieve the aches. But remember that the runny nose is the body's attempt at getting rid of bugs and toxins; the muscle aches and pains are telling you to rest so that the body can concentrate on healing; and the raised temperature aids the body's defences. The medications are unlikely to do much harm, but they may well make the illness last longer.

Cold remedies tend to contain an antihistamine, a cough suppressant or decongestant, and a painkiller. Some may have a stimulant like caffeine to pep you up and a painkiller like aspirin that will make you drowsy; but an aspirin and a cup of tea or coffee would be just as effective – if, indeed, this is the desired effect.

Congestion

Mucus is produced in the nose to trap dust, germs, etc. When irritation causes over-production, and especially if the mucus becomes infected, stuffiness, a full nose and phlegm are the result. This unpleasant stuff is then blown down the nose, coughed up or swallowed, all three being ways of getting rid of the bugs.

We often use drugs to dry up the protective secretions. Not only does this mean we are less able to deal with the germs, but the drugs may also produce various side effects, such as drowsiness, dryness, dizziness, nausea and palpitations. Furthermore, they often dry up secretions in the rest of the body. Many such decongestants or cold remedies also contain phenylephrine hydrochloride, which is a particularly bad mixer with other chemicals; it is not advised for pregnant women, children or anyone with heart problems.

To ease congested sinuses, inhalations and vapour rubs are far more effective, as long as you don't mind smelling of methanol and camphor.

Coughs

Coughing is a normal reflex action for getting rid of lodged food or objects, and for loosening and removing phlegm and the invading bugs trapped within it. It is also used to warn us of any irritants in the air, e.g. smoke.

Cough medicines suppress this vital reflex, which means that, again, we are less able to deal with the invading bugs. They also often contain quite a lot of alcohol, and may have an antihistamine as well, both of which cause drowsiness. So beware of driving under the influence of cough medicine, as it may put you over the limit.

Sucking is a good, natural way of relieving a persistent cough, as it increases saliva production, keeping the mouth and throat moist. A sick child's cough may be soothed by encouraging him to suck a clean thumb.

Sore throat
Salt-and-water or alcohol gargles are very effective at soothing a sore throat, as is sucking, while very cold drinks or lollies soothe any inflammation in the throat.

CUTS AND MINOR WOUNDS

Many antiseptic creams cause skin irritation on sensitive people, and their application may even delay healing. Liquid antiseptics are preferable, although washing with salt and water or with alcohol is just as effective and less likely to cause a skin reaction. Antiseptic wipes are useful if you are away from a source of clean water.

Plasters, too, may delay healing, especially if they are the waterproof type, which can make the tissues surrounding a cut go soggy. Dressings which allow air through are preferable, but they should be removed as soon as possible. Some plasters cause skin rashes. If a plaster is not really needed, don't bother. A cut will usually bleed to clean itself, and will then form its own protective dressing over the wound in the form of a scab, which allows optimum healing.

BURNS

Smothering burns with a soothing or antiseptic cream is,

at best, a waste of time. The quicker you can cool any burn the better; cool the burn immediately with cold water, but if milk, beer or lemonade are nearer than the tap, use these first and then get to water. (Don't on any account put alcohol on to flames.) If it's a bad burn, keep the area immersed in cool water for at least 10 minutes; burns carry on causing damage after they have been removed from the source of the heat, so fast cooling is the essential first step. Then get help if it's needed.

First-degree burns may be painful, but will usually heal without scarring; application of a little vitamin E oil may help after thorough cooling. Second-degree burns blister due to the deeper tissue damage, as tissues try to accumulate water.

Always remove any jewellery around a burn right away, for two reasons.
- Metal jewellery will retain heat, and so will carry on burning.
- Swelling is likely to occur in the healing process; jewellery not removed immediately may have to be cut off later.

LAXATIVES

These must be some of the most abused medicines. Their use is sometimes necessary after operations, childbirth or a period of bed rest, but some people tend to take them daily as a matter of routine, just in case. They should only be used in the short term, when necessary, otherwise they may become essential; the normal body mechanism becomes lazy and unable to cope without its daily dose, and constipation then becomes the norm, or, at the other extreme, watery stools, wind and abdominal pains.

A change in diet is often all that is needed – eating a diet high in fresh fruit, vegetables and whole grains is the best way to avoid constipation, and to be healthy into the bargain. Yet people seem to find this much more difficult and less desirable than taking a tablet or a swig of medicine.

Some laxatives are better than others, but the ones that do the least harm are the ones which are no more than roughage in a pill or drink. Salts are reasonably effective, magnesium salts like milk of magnesia (magnesium hydroxide) usually being better than sodium salts like Epsom salts (many people are likely to be deficient in magnesium, whereas most people already have quite enough sodium). The main problem with salts is that they can upset the balance of minerals in the body.

Lubricants are certainly not the best choice, unless it is for a short period of time only and they are taken to alleviate something like an anal fissure or piles. Liquid paraffin shouldn't be used; certainly, it may work, in that it does the job it is intended to do, but it prevents normal absorption of the fat-soluble vitamins and, besides, it is not really edible.

Other laxatives work by forcing the muscular action of the gut, and shouldn't really be used. Castor oil shouldn't be used at all, especially by pregnant women, in whom it could induce premature labour. These strong purgatives can damage the gut; in particular, they include those laxatives containing senna and phenolphthalein. Some laxatives merely contain soap!

DIARRHOEA

At the other end of the scale you can buy 'thickening medicine'.

Diarrhoea can be caused by nervousness; by some prescription drugs, such as antibiotics; by some illnesses; and by infection, especially food poisoning. Diarrhoea is thus a body signal that it wants to get rid of something, and the quicker the better. Trying to retain this unwanted stuff hardly seems to be the best way to deal with the situation; putting up with the diarrhoea for a while would seem more sensible.

It is not a good idea to use any anti-diarrhoea agent containing choquinol. Kaolin and morphine mixture is a very common remedy for diarrhoea, but as it contains aluminium it is not advisable to take it too frequently as aluminium is a cumulative poison.

Perhaps surprisingly, when you have diarrhoea it is necessary to drink a lot of fluid to make up for the fluids that are lost, and so prevent any dehydration. It is also worth remembering that you are unlikely to be absorbing anything from the gut effectively whilst you have diarrhoea; this includes prescription medicines and, in particular, the pill – a woman should be aware that another form of contraception is needed for the rest of her cycle if she has diarrhoea.

ANTACIDS

Another common and painful digestive disorder is indigestion. We spend millions of pounds every year on antacids, so what do they do and what are the side effects?

Basically antacids neutralise any acid in the stomach and so relieve the burning caused by excess acid. Some may contain substances such as dimethicone; one way or another, these will give you wind as part of their indigestion relief, making big bubbles out of all the little bubbles that are formed in the body's attempt to digest the offending cocktail. Not to be recommended for dinner parties!

Some antacids contain a pain reliever, like aspirin, to go with an acid-reducing chemical. They are usually effective when a simple antacid isn't, but they tend to indicate that it isn't an antacid that is needed.

Many antacids contain aluminium salts, which can cause cumulative problems, and are therefore not advisable in the long term. Some may appear to be free of aluminium while in fact containing it, e.g. magnesium trisilicate contains aluminium hydroxide. Magnesium hydroxide is probably one of the best choices of antacid, as most of us could do with extra magnesium. Sodium hydroxide, i.e. baking powder, is also effective, but does increase the body burden of sodium.

An antacid can certainly be useful on odd occasions of

over-indulgence, but it should not be necessary to take one daily. Antacids do relieve gut pain, but they can easily mask other potentially dangerous conditions. If they are needed daily, it is time to reconsider your diet and food combinations, and to visit the doctor so as to rule out any medical problems.

MOUTH ULCERS

Mouth ulcers are very small white or open ulcers in the mouth. They gain you little sympathy, but feel like Mount Etna erupting on your tongue; they can be very painful, and may make chewing impossible. They often indicate a beta-carotene or zinc deficiency.

Antiseptic rinses are of little value in treating mouth ulcers; they taste awful and kill the good bugs as well as bad ones – and the ulcers aren't usually infected, anyway.

SLIMMING PREPARATIONS

Appetite suppressants are not a good alternative to will-power. Some, containing artificial chemicals, have side effects, while others are nothing more than packaged or tableted roughage. Many contain substances which are either diuretics or laxatives, for obvious reasons.

Powdered, pilled or liquid replacement meals are also not a good idea, for any length of time or, preferably, not at all.

PAIN

A large number of people suffer from severe and recurrent pain and need painkillers almost daily, whilst others take painkillers for the merest twinge. The latter group, would in fact, be better off trying to decide why their body has given them this warning twinge of pain; most people do not appreciate the advantages of pain – the disadvantages always appear more obvious, even though there are advantages. Indeed, we could not live normal lives without the ability to feel pain.

- Gentle pain or sensation is the stimulus that makes us move, whether asleep or awake, when we need to shift our body weight. If we did not move around, our joints and muscles would wear out much more quickly.
- We could easily chew up our own tongues if we couldn't feel the pain when we bit them.
- Pain enables us to avoid more serious injury. For example, pain tells you to get away from a source of heat that is causing you damage, say a hot saucepan that you thoughtlessly picked up.
- Our memory of pain usually ensures that we are discouraged from making the same potentially damaging mistakes again, e.g. picking up a hot saucepan.
- Pain following injury encourages us to rest the damaged part of the body and to judge when it is getting better, or not, as the case might be.
- Pain can be a warning that all is not well, and that you need to take steps to rectify the situation.
- Pain may also warn that all is well, but that you are in for some really heavy work, e.g. a woman in labour.
- Pain often causes us to rub the painful area, causing a local increase in blood circulation. The increased number of white blood cells and extra heat then speeds up the repair of the damaged tissue.

All too often, however, pain appears to have no useful function; it just hurts. Painkillers (analgesics), will certainly reduce the pain, but they don't cure the cause; the body should therefore be used very carefully when painkillers are being taken, so as not to inflict any further damage.

Morphine

Morphine relieves pain more effectively than anything else. It is the main active ingredient of opium, and comes from the poppy. It was appropriately named after Morpheus, the Greek god of dreams.

Morphine should only be used when necessary and under strict medical supervision. It is a sedative and, like its semi-synthetic derivative heroin, can be addictive if not used properly. It is included in very small amounts in over-the-counter medicines like kaolin and morphine, where it is supposed to take the tummy pain out of diarrhoea.

Codeine
Codeine, in an effective dose, is a prescription drug derived from opium, but it is a weaker painkiller than morphine. It could be addictive if used for a long time, and a side effect may be constipation. In conjunction with aspirin, it is considered to be more effective at removing pain than by using either drug alone.

It is very important to remember that all of the opiates cause drowsiness, and it is not advisable to drive, etc., whilst taking them.

Aspirin
Aspirin was originally derived from the willow tree, and along with paracetamol, is one of our oldest, safest and most effective painkillers. It is thought to act by blocking the production of one of the groups of prostaglandins.

There are, nevertheless, a number of side effects associated with aspirin; some people, for example, are sensitive to all salicylates, while others get dizziness, headache or ringing in the ears when they use it a lot. The most common problem is that overuse can cause irritation or bleeding in the gut; this is minimised by using soluble aspirin, although it is unfortunate that the soluble form usually contains saccharine for flavouring.

There are many variations on the aspirin and paracetamol theme, all of which have other additives. Some contain aluminium and are definitely not advised on a regular basis. It is worth remembering that the more ingredients there are, the more likely these are to react together and to produce side effects.

Alternative suggestions for alleviating pain
Painkillers do not usually cure the problem, but

unfortunately they are sometimes necessary. It goes without saying that the best way to deal with pain is to find the cause and remove it, although this is not always possible. There are, in fact, many ways of dealing with pain; they can be used on their own in some cases, or in conjunction with painkillers, perhaps enabling a reduction in dosage for long-term users.

To begin with, pain can be both mental and/or physical, and our threshold for coping with either varies from person to person – even from day to day – depending on our attitude, whether we are happy or sad, winning or losing, worried or afraid, determined or depressed.

- If aspirin brings relief, it may be possible to gain the same relief, in the long term, by altering the diet. Aspirin blocks prostaglandins derived from arachidonic acid. By increasing the essential fatty acid linoleic acid (found in sunflower and safflower oils and seeds), and at the same time reducing saturated fat and meat, production of less inflammatory prostaglandins are favoured whilst the arachidonic acid pathway is reduced. This is particularly the case for arthritics, who can often gain a lot of relief by drastically reducing meat consumption and including cod liver oil and cold-pressed sunflower or safflower oils in the daily diet.

- We have two main types of nerve fibres, thick ones and thin ones. Thick fibres carry messages to the brain or spinal cord quickly; they convey pleasure, touch, rubbing, and tickling sensations. Pain is conveyed more slowly in the thin fibres. The central nervous system can only respond to a certain number of messages, after which all the others are lost. Because of this, touch can 'dilute' intense pain; to rub or massage a painful area stimulates the thick fibres, so less of the slower painful thin fibres get their messages through. Acupuncture and acupressure may also bring relief. Similarly a vibrator may bring relief if applied bear to or on the painful spot, whilst a comfortable rocking chair may do wonders for a bad back.

- Relief from some pain can be found by temperature

change – a hot bath or hot water bottle, or alternatively an ice pack.

- Exercise is good for some chronic pain, though obviously not if you have just broken a leg. Exercise causes the release of endorphins, which are natural brain chemicals, similar to opiates, that induce a sense of well-being.

- Relaxation and laughter are also important in coping with pain. Relaxation helps to relieve tension in muscles, and laughter helps to restore morale. Concentrating on a good book, television programme, music or other hobby will also lessen pain, and is definitely preferable to lying in bed thinking about the pain.

Mental pain is not as obvious to an outsider as physical pain, but it can be just as distressing. Keeping busy and distracting your thoughts from the painful ones can be a good way of dealing with this sort of pain, although it should not be bottled up or ignored all of the time. Massage is also good, as we tend to store toxic chemicals produced during emotional pain in our muscles; massage can help to disperse these, as can exercise, while the latter will also cause the production of endorphins. Positive coping with emotional pain, preferably with support from family and friends, is better than sinking into the tranquilliser trap.

TRANQUILLISERS

Tranquillisers are addictive drugs, and are bad for your health. I can say nothing new about them; I can only express my firm view that they have caused more pain and suffering than they have relieved.

Stress can cause many people very great problems if they cannot deal with it effectively. More and more is expected of us in less and less time. We are encouraged to worry, to watch the clock, to hurry and to be able to cope with any and every problem that comes along, but are tranquillisers and sleeping pills that belong to the benzodiazepine group any help? There are hundreds of these drugs on the market and some people are more sensitive than others to their effects.

What do they do?

Benzodiazepines are hypnotic sedatives and muscle relaxants. They have been used to tame wild animals, but most research shows that they increase aggressive behaviour in humans. Once ingested, they are absorbed by our body fat, so the amount of body fat we carry may well be a factor in our dosage requirements and sensitivity to the drugs.

- They make you feel sleepy.
- They alter the rhythm of the electrical activity in the brain.
- They relax tense muscles, whether you want them relaxed all of the time or not.
- They alter the body's production of hormones and neurotransmitters, so affecting mood. This may relieve anxiety in the short term, but, ironically, in the long term increases depression.
- They are addictive. As the weeks go by, greater doses are needed for the same effect.
- They are not easy substances for the body to get rid of; it takes quite a while after discontinuing the drugs before their breakdown products are removed from the body. These products keep accumulating all the time the drugs are being taken.
- There is also increasing concern that tranquillisers may speed up the growth of cancerous cells, although it is difficult to tell whether it is the tranquillisers that cause the growth of the cancer or the reaction of the individual to the problems and stresses for which he is being treated.

Possible side effects

There are many side effects attributable to the taking of tranquillisers, although they will vary from person to person.

- They make you less efficient.

- Concentration wanders.
- You may feel tired and lethargic most of the time.
- You may forget important (and trivial) things.
- There may be a loss of long-term memory.
- Balance may be altered, causing unsteadiness or dizziness.
- A loss of interest in sex is common.
- There may be a loss of interest in most things, or even in living in general.
- Thoughts and actions often become careless.

Absent-mindedness may lead to embarrassing situations, like forgetting car keys; forgetting to pick up the children at the right time; forgetting an appointment; forgetting where you parked the car; forgetting to take the house keys with you before you close the front door; or even being stopped for shoplifting because you have picked something up to look at it and, without thinking, haven't put it down before leaving the shop. Tranquillisers may cause you to worry about whether you are in control or not; about whether you are going to do anything silly; whether you have your pills with you; whether you have enough left; whether you have already taken one and so should or shouldn't take another.

Dangers

Tranquillisers are an obvious danger to the individual taking them because they may cause addiction and antisocial behaviour, as well as increase the risk of accident. They are only going to add to an over-stressed or anxious person's problems if he or she is arrested for shoplifting (albeit unintentional), or causes a car accident; they will then have to live with the consequences of these actions for the rest of their life, whereas the original problems may well fade away.

There is also a danger to society in general, as people taking tranquillisers have little emotional response; they often accept things without question and don't communicate effectively with family or friends, so causing frustration in those around them, even though they themselves may feel that life is comfortable and undemanding.

As has been explained, it is dangerous to drive whilst taking these drugs, as the risk of a road accident is five times greater than normal. Indeed, in Australia it is an offence to drive if you are taking tranquillisers. It is also not advisable to use any other type of machinery which could cause damage, even at home, as the risk of an accident is so greatly increased.

Furthermore, benzodiazepines react with other drugs – even with our common ones like tea, coffee and alcohol. They are obviously not advisable during pregnancy or whilst breastfeeding; their use for a young mother, unable to cope, is more likely to increase her inability, as well as to increase the likelihood of her being violent towards her baby if they are continued for long.

For all of these reasons, tranquillisers should only be taken, if at all, under strict medical supervision and never on repeat prescription.

Withdrawal
The problems of withdrawal from tranquillisers should never be under-estimated. Tranquillisers should certainly not be stopped suddenly.

Symptoms of withdrawal may include shaking, dizziness, forgetfulness, nausea, panic attacks, headaches, loss of self-confidence, sweating, crying, excessive thirst and, ironically, sleeplessness and depression, i.e. the very problems the tranquillisers were supposed to help. It is therefore not a good idea for anyone living alone either to take or, more particularly, to try to withdraw from, tranquillisers.

As tranquillisers merely hide symptoms and do not cure either anxiety or insomnia in the long term, is it worth polluting your inner environment and risking the consequences? Surely it is better to reach out to other people, at least as a first effort? Often the sufferer bottles things up and hides the problems, so that their friends do not realise that help is needed, but there is almost always someone available to help if they know that there is a problem.

GENERAL ADVICE ON MEDICINES

Think about the medicines you take, and use only the ones that you need. If you have medicines in the house, remember these very basic rules:

- Read the ingredients and instructions.
- Don't exceed the advised dosage.
- If you are forgetful, make a note of the time whenever you take any medicine, so that you don't double dose.
- Don't mix medicines unless your doctor says it's all right.
- Don't drink alcohol if you are taking medicines.
- Be careful driving, etc., preferably don't.
- Don't take medication if you are pregnant.
- Don't use unprescribed medication for babies.
- Don't self-medicate for longer than 5–7 days.
- Don't use out of date medication, unlabelled medication or anything that has been prescribed for someone else.

If you are not sure ... don't.

CONCLUSION

29
HOPE FOR THE FUTURE

At present we are living dangerously, often oblivious to personal and domestic pollution, and often detached from global environmental problems.

On a macro-environmental level, man has sometimes irresponsibly, and sometimes unintentionally, poisoned or polluted the world, and it is now showing obvious symptoms of disease. We all share this world with one another, and we all therefore have an obligation to correct the mistakes, to clean up pollution and to pass on our planet in good condition to future generations. Fortunately this is now being recognised and steps are being taken to re-establish a natural balance.

On a micro-environmental level, however, most of us spend the greater part of our lives in one building or another, and it is only just being recognised that the materials used to build and furnish these buildings, as well as the conditions within the buildings themselves, can contribute significantly to environmental illness. Fortunately we can correct most of these problems with a little thought and knowledge. But those in the building and decorating trades still need to be made more aware of the effects on health of the materials that they use. Such materials should be clearly labelled with exactly what chemicals they are liable to contain. We have the technology to build comfortable and safe homes and places of work. When building them, thought should be given not only to energy conservation, but also to chemical and electromagnetic pollution. We need to consider cost in terms of health as well as in terms of money.

Individual good health depends to a large extent on the

level of our own personal pollution. We cannot control how other people think, but we are in charge of our own thoughts; we cannot dictate what other people eat, but we can choose, to some extent, what we put into our own mouths. The provision of nutritious food and drink, free from unnecessary chemicals and as low as possible in those additives that are, perhaps, sometimes necessary, for example, preservatives, should be a national priority; after all, a country's main asset is its population.

We have more knowledge now than ever before. If this knowledge is put to constructive rather than destructive use, we should be able to achieve the optimum standard of living and health. It needs to be realised, however, that we have to live in a state of equilibrium with our environment; we cannot just use and abuse it and expect to escape the consequences. Every effort needs to be made to deter polluters – of every kind – from ruining our earth.

In restoring this necessary natural balance, the way we spend our lives is thus of far more importance than the way we spend our money. Our environment, just as much as we ourselves, can only take so much pollution; if we exceed that environmental or personal tolerance level, breakdown is inevitable – and often swift. There is, however, hope for the future, as long as we all care enough to make it happen. There is a lot we could do to improve our resistance to disease and quality of life if only we all knew how to avoid, or minimise the effects of, so many of the things that are causing sick people and a sick earth.